W9-CCD-279

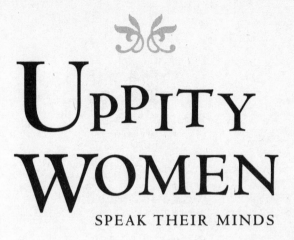

UPPITY WOMEN

SPEAK THEIR MINDS

Quotes from little-known vixens and
forgotten boat rockers to famous trailblazers,
troublemakers, and headline grabbers

VICKI LEÓN

MJF BOOKS ❧ NEW YORK

Published by MJF Books
Fine Communications
322 Eighth Avenue
New York, NY 10001

Uppity Women Speak Their Minds
LC Control Number: 2015909754
ISBN 978-1-60671-315-0

Designed by Lisa Chovnick

Printed in the United States of America.

MJF Books and the MJF colophon are trademarks
of Fine Creative Media, Inc.

QF   10   9   8   7   6   5   4   3

CONTENTS

FOR MARY DAVIS

And with special thanks to: David Forrer,
Nathaniel Jacks, the MJF crew, Sabrina Testa,
the splendid Morro Bay Library staff, and
the uppity women who left us the
gift of their vivid words

INTRODUCTION

THIRTY YEARS ago, while researching and writing the first of nine books about uppity women worldwide and throughout history, I began to recognize what these ladies had in common. From girls to grannies, queens to slaves, all shared key qualities that made them worth knowing, and worth hearing about as trailblazers and role models. No matter what their status, these women spoke their minds, often at great personal cost. Luckily for us, their words have been preserved in various ways. There are sassy remarks on cuneiform clay tablets; defiant one-liners in letters and diaries; surprising sound bites in speeches, telegrams, and newspapers; and wicked witticisms within books written by them or about them.

When my historical detective work began, what women did was vastly easier to find than what they said. Although quotations are more accessible today, references such as *Bartlett's Familiar Quotations* still give quotes by females a paltry amount of coverage.

Unlike other quotation books you'll find, this one has more than a bare-bones selection of "she saids." Each of the 170 entries includes one or more paragraphs providing context for a deeper understanding of the quotation and the woman quoted.

The wit and wisdom rolling off these saucy tongues covers a huge span of time and geography, from ancient Egypt to Asia, from early Europe to the colonization of the Americas, and onward into the 20th century.

You'll encounter plenty of insight, insult, and cleverness from these women, but their most memorable words also bring to life their courageous campaigns for human dignity, including fights to end slavery, stop wars, gain workers' rights, and win legal and voting rights for women.

Gathered here, speaking their minds, revealing their true feelings, these unquenchably uppity women vividly remind us of where we've been and how far indeed we have come.

* * * *

This book contains well-known and notorious names, plus a great many unsung women, whose words will shock, awe, and delight. Rather than organize these outspoken females in conventional ways, this book groups them into seven sections by the nature of their accomplishments, which add up to a definition of uppity women:

1. *Brains and Brass.* Lively, inquiring minds that thirsted for knowledge, higher education, and meaningful work.

2. *Hooked on Passion and Power.* High-vitality personalities, passionate about power and politics.

3. *Warriors for a Rainbow of Rights.* Compassionate warriors who actively fought for others' human rights as well as their own.

4. *Unfettered Is Better.* Independent female spirits whose goals were sometimes achieved by going solo, through all of life or part of it.

5. *Soul Mates and Odd Couples.* Dedicated women, often anchored by love and devotion to family and mates, sometimes in "opposites attract" relationships.

6. *Risk Takers and Roamers.* Bold risk takers whose humor helped them navigate through life's journey.

7. *Dilemmas, Close Calls, and Dire Straits.* Pioneers with hang-in-there gumption, who explored difficult new worlds, fought unusual foes, and sometimes, gallantly went down in flames.

UPPITY WOMEN

SPEAK THEIR MINDS

CHAPTER ONE

BRAINS AND BRASS

Mary Astell

ca. 1666–ca. 1715

A MIDDLE-CLASS British lass, Mary Astell received a thumping-good education, funded by a clearly quirky uncle. In turn, Mary got the bizarre notion that all girls should receive similar help.

> *"Since God has given women as well as men intelligent souls, why should they be forbidden to improve them?"*

Astell's proposal to train young female minds was a mash-up of Protestant convent and scholarly academy; it was met with scorn. The final outcome? A bishop launched his "own" idea, a transparent filching of Mary's plan.

LADY MURASAKI

CA. 978-1025

ALL SHE wanted was to learn the same cool stuff her brother did. Dad came down hard on her for spying on her brother's Chinese lessons—and slipping him the answers. The Japanese girl who would one day be known as Lady Murasaki wrote in her diary:

> *"It wasn't long before I repented of having distinguished myself. Even boys become unpopular if it's discovered they are fond of their books. For a girl, it's worse."*

Rebellious, she continued her Chinese studies in secret. Even more outrageous, she began writing a romance, *The Tale of Genji*. Her 1,100-page masterpiece would become the world's first novel. Her diary is still treasured for its honesty.

LUCY STONE

1818–1893

LUCY STONE chalked up several superlatives, starting with being the first woman from Massachusetts to earn a bachelor's degree. As a new Oberlin College grad, Stone jumped into public speaking, soon scoring raves for her dynamic talks on abolition and women's rights issues.

Lucy also accumulated groupies, including a persistent social reformer, Henry Blackwell. For years, Blackwell argued with her publicly, while proposing privately. In 1855, she finally agreed to marry him—but only if he agreed to a list of conditions concerning equality.

The contract, which Stone drew up, specified keeping her own surname, which American women had routinely forfeited upon marriage. As the new Mrs. Lucy Stone affirmed:

"My name is my identity and must not be lost."

Women would later found the Lucy Stone League, taking her pledge as their motto.

AMELIA JENKS BLOOMER
1818–1894

MOSTLY REMEMBERED (with a snicker) for inventing bloomers, Amelia Bloomer was farsighted—and into comfort. The getup she urged women to wear resembled harem pants with a short overskirt. American men were aghast, insisting the Bible was anti-bloomer. Most women of the time continued to struggle into 20- to 40-pound hoop skirts and heavyweight dresses.

Apparel aside, Bloomer lent an intelligent voice to bigger matters. When legislators decreed that married women "did not have free and independent souls" and therefore no right to own property, Amelia went ballistic, writing a scathing editorial in *The Lily* newspaper and revealing these male actions to a national audience:

"Man legislates for us and now holds himself accountable for us! How kind of him, and what a weight is lifted from us!"

EMMA LAZARUS

1849–1887

BORN INTO an affluent Sephardic family, Emma began writing poetry while a teenager, and later became interested in Zionism and persecuted immigrants:

"The Jewish Question . . . has gradually absorbed more and more of my mind and heart."

The group that began raising funds to pay for a pedestal for New York's new Statue of Liberty asked Lazarus to write something. She meditated on that motherly figure holding a torch to welcome humanity. Her 14-line sonnet, "The New Colossus" (which was not read at the statue's dedication), includes these compassionate, unforgettable words:

*"Give me your tired, your poor,
Your huddled masses yearning to breathe free."*

Elizabeth Heyssin

active 1596–1602

In 16th-century Germany, legal wrath was often aimed at female barber-surgeons. One of these was Dr. Elizabeth Heyssin, a blameless medico who had been successful enough to place her own daughter in medical training.

Just as the male doctors did, Heyssin made house calls, wrote prescriptions, and sniffed urine. In 1596, however, her fellow sawbones tried to yank her practice by taking her to court. A multiyear litigation began. Elizabeth's rebuttal won her case:

"Such activities are done by honorable women, not only here but in other cities as large and important as Memmingen. Such are fitting things for women to do."

SACAGAWEA

CA. 1788–1812

THE LEWIS and Clark expedition of 1804–6 met success thanks to a certain measure of female savvy. The two leaders would not have had documentation for their discoveries had it not been for Sacagawea. After a boat capsized, it was she who made the risky rescue of their journals from a raging river.

Moreover, the presence of a baby-toting native woman discouraged hostiles from attacking; and her plant knowledge warded off hunger and disease. Sacagawea also spoke languages her co-travelers did not, enabling the party to obtain horses at a critical point.

As far as we know, Sacagawea complained only once during her 6,000-mile round trip. While camped near the Pacific, Clark quoted her in his journal:

"She'd traveled a long way to see the great waters and now that a monstrous fish [a beached whale] was also to be seen, she thought it very hard that she could not . . . see them."

Despite dreary rains, Clark took her to the seashore, a fitting gift for all she'd done.

CASSANDRA FEDELE

CA. 1465–1558

WHIP-SMART Cassandra Fedele got a Champagne education. A multilingual wunderkind at 12, she became the pride of Venice. Her recitations were standing-room only; her fan mail from big names was copious.

After reveling in scholarly stardom, Fedele—faced with the social liability that accompanies spinsterdom—dutifully married a doctor. She logged 16 years of childless wedlock before losing all possessions, including husband, in a shipwreck.

The new widow returned to literature, her projects now consisting of letters to each new pope, pleading for a job.

As she neared 90, Cassandra again became an interesting prodigy. Invited to deliver a speech before the queen of Poland, Cassandra recycled her now-vintage material about the rewards of scholarship:

> *"Even if the study of literature offers women no honors, I believe women must nonetheless . . . embrace such studies for the pleasure . . . they contain."*

ELIZABETH BLACKWELL

1821-1910

BORN IN England, Elizabeth Blackwell loved history and planned to teach. Medical school was not in her plans. Frankly, she hated the notion:

"The thought of dwelling on the physical structure of the body and its various ailments filled me with disgust."

But Blackwell had a change of heart when a dear friend fell fatally ill. After her cancer attacked the reproductive organs, the woman insisted that her suffering would have been far less had her doctor been a woman.

Admitted to Geneva Medical College, Elizabeth got her license but met steely resistance from male doctors. Not about to turn tail, in 1853 Dr. Blackwell started her own ob-gyn clinic for women in New York. Later, besides training nurses during the Civil War and opening her own medical school (females only), at 53 she crossed the Atlantic to join the teaching staff of England's first school of medicine for women.

MARY GODWIN SHELLEY

1797–1851

EIGHTEEN-YEAR-OLD Mary Godwin was hanging out with lover Percy Shelley and other literary friends at Lake Geneva, when storms confined the gang indoors. Inhaling wine and laudanum, they competed to see who could pen the best horror story.

Mary won, using as the plotline a ghastly nightmare she'd just had. Encouraged by future husband Percy, she lengthened her story into a book, and three years later, it was published. A best seller, it chilled audiences and continues to do so.

She called it *Frankenstein, or The Modern Prometheus.* Its plot was partly inspired by electrical experiments scientists were performing on dead and living tissue in her day. Shelley's goal?

"A tale to make the reader dread to look around, to curdle the blood and quicken the beatings of the heart."

Maggie Lena Walker

1864–1934

In 1903, this remarkable woman made an unusual pitch to her fellow citizens of the black community of Richmond, Virginia:

> *"Let us put our money together; let us use our*
> *money—and reap the benefit ourselves."*

Her audience agreed, and Maggie Lena Walker established the Saint Luke Penny Savings Bank. Such a bank was sorely needed. For decades after the Civil War, blacks had no place to go for home or business loans. As its head, Mrs. Walker became the first African American female bank president in the nation. Banking was only a part of Walker's economic development plan. High-energy Maggie also launched other start-ups, including a community newspaper.

VINNIE REAM HOXIE

1847–1914

"With trembling hands [I] had taken the proportions of the figure from the blood-stained garments President Lincoln had worn on that last and fearful night."

Vinnie Ream, a young artist from the Wisconsin wilderness, spoke those words in a speech to Congress. Earlier, in 1864–65, she had spent five months with President Lincoln, who sat for her each morning. The teen had won a competition to sculpt his likeness.

After the assassination, a shocked Congress commissioned a life-size statue of the fallen president. Thanks to her superlative work, Vinnie again was chosen. She spent several years in Europe, choosing the marble and carving the statue, unveiled with emotional ceremony in 1871.

After marriage, Vinnie Ream Hoxie continued to sculpt, creating her own legacy. Like Lincoln, she'd been born in a log cabin and had come a long, long way.

PRUDENCE CRANDALL

1803–1890

"Then let it [the school] sink. I will not dismiss her!"

Those were the fighting words of a stouthearted teacher who ran a fancy school for girls. Invited to start an academy by upscale Connecticut residents, Prudence admitted a black teen in 1831. White parents had a fit, yanking their girls out.

Crandall coolly changed gears, advertising her school "for young ladies and little misses of color." Gutsy students enrolled, but the academy was terrorized by pistol-firing and entrails-slinging protestors. The ugly acts of racism extended to charges against Crandall and several trials, which she ultimately won. Malicious harassment continued, however, until Crandall finally left the area.

After the Civil War, Connecticut's legislature shamefacedly repealed the Black Law—which claimed that free African Americans were not actually citizens—and granted the now-elderly Crandall an annual $400 pension, and an apology. Crandall had failed in her mission to provide an education for her students, but she had taught the town a lesson.

ABIGAIL SCOTT DUNIWAY

1834–1915

A SALARIED teacher when she met her future husband, Abigail Duniway became a pioneer, mother, and farmer. While tending to countless unpaid chores, she made thousands of pounds of butter to sell. Yet when her husband lost their Oregon farm through unwise business decisions, Abigail was helpless to intervene. The trauma radicalized her:

> *"I was my husband's silent partner, a legal nonentity, with no voice or power."*

The family moved to Portland, and she started a progressive weekly newspaper that thrived for 16 years. Editor-publisher Abigail also gave lectures around the Northwest on legal rights for women. In time, she convinced Oregon legislators to give women the power to sue, control their own earnings, and go into business solo. With Duniway's influence, suffrage laws were passed in Idaho, Washington, and finally Oregon.

BATHSUA MAKIN

1612–CA. 1683

A BRITISH teacher-linguist, Bathsua Pell Makin loved to lambaste the male sex. In one of her books (which were not exactly best sellers), she wrote:

> *"Had God intended women only as a finer sort of cattle, He would not have made them reasonable. Brutes, a few degrees higher than Monkies, might have better fitted some men's Lust, Pride, and Pleasure; especially . . . those that desire to keep women ignorant to be tyrannized over."*

Inspired by travels in Holland, where women enjoyed more rights, Makin opened a school for girls that emphasized hard science, history, and languages. She had few illusions, however:

> *"A learned woman is thought to be a comet, that bodes mischief whenever it appears."*

BERTHA VON SUTTNER

1843–1914

IN 1864, Prussians invaded her homeland and gutsy Prague native Bertha von Suttner learned firsthand about war's horrific toll. She published an antiwar novel in 1889 called *Lay Down Your Arms!* It sold hundreds of thousands of copies worldwide; its sales at the time were second only to those of *Uncle Tom's Cabin.*

Von Suttner then spent seven years editing a pacifist journal and corresponding regularly with Alfred Nobel about the peace movement. Before he died, Nobel decided to include a peace prize among his annual awards, possibly motivated by Bertha's inspirational work.

Awarded the Nobel Peace Prize in 1905, its first female recipient, von Suttner declaimed:

"War is not necessary to achieve glory. In technology, art, science . . . more beautiful goals than those on the battlefield beckon."

SARAH UPDIKE GODDARD

CA. 1700–1770

THANK GOODNESS for an industrious daughter, thought Sarah Goddard, a widow with a print shop. With the ingenious Katherine's help, she'd also gotten three newspapers up and running.

Then son William showed up, demanding funds for one of his flaky ventures. Instead of cash, she sent him this exasperated letter:

"I heartily wish it was within the reach of my faint efforts to convey to you what threescore and almost ten years experience has taught me, of the mere nothingness of all [the political hogwash] you are disputing about, and the infinite importance and value of what you thereby neglect and disregard —a jewel of inestimable value."

The jewel in question? The *Providence Gazette*, one of the female Goddards' success stories.

JANE SHARP

CA. 1641–1671

"To the Midwives of England: Sisters,
I have often sat down sad in the consideration
of the many miseries women endure in the
hands of unskillful midwives."

A mince-no-words professional, author and midwife Jane Sharp educated women seeking to be competent midwives. In Europe, males had begun horning in on the work of delivering babies. Most men, however, thought little of hands-on birthing skills. Instead, they swore by the writings of ancient Greco-Romans and their notions of wandering wombs and other harmful ideas about women's physiology and reproduction.

Jane's remedy was *The Compleat Midwife's Companion*, the first book of its kind ever published in English. It has remained in print over the centuries, a comforting, frequently consulted companion.

HARRIOT KEZIA HUNT

1805–1875

A FAN of herbalism, this bright Bostonian had practiced medicine and worked with established doctors for 20 years before applying to the medical program at Harvard University. Harriot Kezia Hunt wanted to attend Harvard to observe dissections and learn more about physiology.

Did her prior experiences open doors at the males-only campus? Nope. Undaunted, six years later Hunt reapplied, her application bolstered by recommendations from such big shots as Oliver Wendell Holmes. This time the student body wrote a whiny manifesto to her. The upshot was, "Get lost!"

Several years later, in her book *Glances and Glimpses*, Harriot lobbed an icily polite putdown:

"The 1851 class of Harvard have purchased for themselves a notoriety they will not covet in years to come."

MARY MASON LYON

1797–1849

"Go where no one else will go; do
what no one else will do."

THESE WORDS sound like something Gloria Steinem would say—but Mary Mason Lyon spoke them two centuries before the feminist icon's birth. The visionary Lyon focused on a goal that sounded ludicrous to her peers: founding a college for women. The Massachusetts native went door-to-door, soliciting donations.

She was 39 by the time she obtained a charter; her Mount Holyoke College opened its doors in 1836. Educator Lyon encouraged middle-class aspirants to join her math- and science-heavy program by keeping yearly fees to a low $64.

Holyoke became the first of America's prestigious Seven Sisters colleges for women. The fire Lyon had kindled was kept ablaze by her graduates, who opened schools of their own in the American West as it was settled.

ANNA ZENGER

ACTIVE 1734

WHEN HER husband, freedom of the press pioneer John Peter Zenger, got thrown behind bars for libel, Anna Zenger grabbed the reins of the *New York Weekly Journal*, which was under attack by the British colonial government. She and other busy matrons had already ruffled feathers with their sweetly belligerent manifesto in the weekly:

> *"We are the housekeepers, pay our taxes,*
> *carry on trade, and most of us are she-merchants,*
> *and as we in some measure contribute to the*
> *support of the government, we ought to be*
> *entitled to some of the sweets of it."*

Widowed a decade later, Zenger competently published the *Journal* for years until her son stepped into the role.

SUSIE KING TAYLOR

1848–1912

SUSIE KING TAYLOR, born in slavery, volunteered as a nurse for her husband's African American regiment when the Civil War began. Having arduously gained literacy, she dedicated herself to educating others. Between battles, she taught soldiers to read.

Later Susie started freedmen's schools on Georgia's barrier islands, and in 1902 completed her memoir of her experiences as America's first black army nurse.

After her second marriage, Mrs. Taylor lived in Boston, returning south once to retrieve her dying son. Heartsick at the continuing malignancy of racism, she wrote:

"We cannot sing 'My country, 'tis of thee, Sweet Land of Liberty!' It is a hollow mockery."

LYDIA MARIA CHILD

1802–1880

LYDIA CHILD came early to the equal-rights table, lambasting slavery and brutality to Native Americans. An unblinking abolitionist and suffrage advocate, she won applause—and audiences—with her crusading style and humor.

> *"We first crush people to the earth, and then claim the right of trampling on them forever, because they are prostrate."*

Child was a woman of stamina and versatility, and authored 47 books. Novelistically, she portrayed rigid Puritanism and witch-craft obsessions with surgical accuracy. Between novels, she whipped out nonfiction. Perennially poor, she wrote a blunt how-to for other impoverished housewives, an evergreen book that sold for decades. Child also edited the first American magazine for children, for which she composed poetry, including the still-popular verse that begins:

> *"Over the river and through the wood, to grandmother's house we go."*

LOUISE LABÉ

CA. 1520–1566

LIFE IN 16th-century France overflowed with risks and restrictions. Ebullient Louise Labé believed, however, that women could learn or do anything. As proof, she got a marvelous education, took up jousting and martial arts, and still found time for marriage and discreet affairs. Louise wrote poetry and prose, held her own at the famous salon she hosted, and penned fearless challenges to girlfriends:

"Since a time has come . . . when the severe laws of men no longer prevent women from applying themselves to the sciences and other disciplines . . . those of us who can, should use this long-craved freedom . . . to let men see how greatly they wronged us when depriving us of its honor and advantages."

ELIZABETH TIMOTHY

CA. 1710–1757

ONE CHRISTMAS season in South Carolina, the Timothy family's weekly newspaper was on shaky ground, and matriarch Elizabeth was about to give birth to her seventh child. Then her husband died. Between labor pains, Elizabeth wrote and rewrote the lead for the next issue:

"Whereas the late Printer of this Gazette hath been deprived of his life by an unhappy Accident, I take this opportunity of informing the Publick, that I shall continue the Paper as usual. . . . [Readers] will be kindly pleased to continue their Favours . . . to his poor afflicted Widow with six small children and another hourly expected."

That poignant "hourly expected" did the trick; subscriptions grew gratifyingly. Sharper at promotion and economics than her dearly departed, one of America's first female publishers enjoyed a long and profitable run.

CHAPTER TWO

HOOKED ON PASSION
AND POWER

CATHERINE THE GREAT

1729–1796

QUEEN CATHERINE II of Russia, known as Catherine the Great, got away with quite a lot during her 34-year reign, from maintaining a string of disposable lovers to throne-jumping her husband, Peter the not-so-Great.

Brainy but hard as nails, the queen was famous for saying:

"I shall be an autocrat: that's my trade. And the good Lord will forgive me: that's His."

CATHERINE OF SIENA

CA. 1350–1380

AN ITALIAN mystic, Catherine of Siena attracted huge numbers of devotees, thanks to her bizarre and ghastly acts of piety, which ranged from undergoing flagellation three times daily to drinking the pus of plague victims.

A pope-badgering diplomat and advocate for the Crusades, she had spunk and wit. One example of the latter can be seen in her remark to the queen of Naples:

"Sometimes, God works through rascally men, in order that they may execute justice on His enemy."

CATERINA SFORZA

1463–1509

LIVING THE virago lifestyle in late medieval Italy was no picnic. Smoking hot, sharp-tongued, aggression-loving noble-woman Caterina Sforza spent years, starting when she was a preteen and even while heavily pregnant, defending her lands and fighting popes, Borgias, and other male menaces. At their hands she endured a brutal, assault-filled prison term, during which she wrote copiously to keep sane.

To her priestly confessor, Caterina made an eerie, *Godfather*-like threat:

> *"Could I write all, the world*
> *would turn to stone."*

AGRIPPINA THE YOUNGER

CA. AD 15-59

CHILDBIRTH IN imperial Rome was greeted not with baby showers but with omens aplenty. Married three times, once to her own uncle, Agrippina had one dream: to see her only child, a little fellow called Nero, rule Rome.

An astrologer read her newborn's horoscope and gave her the good news/bad news forecast: her son would either become emperor or he would commit matricide.

A powermonger who knew you had to pay to play, she snapped, "*Occidat dum imperet!*" In other words:

*"As long as he becomes emperor,
let him kill me!"*

CLEOPATRA

69–31 BC

THE MOST loved and hated queen of ancient times, Cleopatra VII of Egypt was Macedonian, like Alexander the Great. Logging 21 years of solo rule, Cleo also entered into strategic marriages to start her own dynasty.

While there has been much written about her, nothing authentic *from* her was known until 2001, when a document from 33 BC surfaced that gave a royal tax exemption to one of Mark Antony's commanders. It was a sweet deal: no taxes on property, plus wine imports would be tax-free forever.

Countersigned in Greek, in what is now confirmed to be Cleopatra's hand, it says:

"Make it so!"

It sounds right for the super-efficient ruler she must have been, doesn't it?

PHARAOH HATSHEPSUT

CA. 1503–1483 BC

ALTHOUGH CLEOPATRA VII deserves her kudos, the stand-out among Egypt's handful of female rulers was Hatshepsut. She not only kept her homeland out of wars, she carried out ambitious building programs.

Among her superb edifices were twin obelisks. One remains in place in the temple complex of Karnak, a stunner in red granite. For posterity, proud Hatshepsut had these almost wistful words carved into the stone:

"Now my heart turns to and fro,
In thinking what will the people say,
They who shall see my monument in after years,
And shall speak of what I have done."

BOUDICCA OF THE ICENI

CA. AD 30–CA. 60

ONE OF the wildcat warrior women who fought the Roman Empire and bloodied it temporarily, this tall redhead was co-leader of the Iceni tribe of ancient Britain. After killing her mate, the Romans flogged Boudicca and assaulted her teenage daughters—a big mistake. She immediately hustled military support from other tribes in Britain. She got it, after taking some sharp digs at male courage:

"It is not as a woman descended from noble ancestry, but as one of the people I am avenging lost freedom, my scourged body, the outraged chastity of my daughters. In this battle, you must conquer or die. This is a woman's resolve; as for men, they may live and be slaves."

MARIE-ANTOINETTE

1755–1793

BOOED BY the French, who dubbed her the "Austrian canine," Viennese teen Marie-Antoinette got into deeper hot water when her barely virile husband became King Louis XVI. She needed distractions. Was it her fault that the only decent place to throw parties and gamble was the Palace of Versailles? You'd think people, even starving peasants, would cut her some slack. A little pampering, *s'il vous plaît.*

On October 16, 1793, the peasants got quite a show. Marie-Antoinette's visit to the guillotine drew more than 200,000 spectators. Her sign-off was defiant:

"The moment when my ills are going to end is not the moment when courage is going to fail me."

Queen Henrietta Maria
1609–1666

HENRIETTA MARIA of France was a petite 15-year-old when she boarded a ship to cross the English Channel to marry stumpy little Charles I of England. The stormy crossing panicked the crew, but Henrietta remained calm, scornfully commenting:

"Queens of England are never drowned."

But queens do get returned to France like dirty laundry. In 1642, devoutly Catholic Henrietta got the heave-ho. An antiroyalist bunch didn't much like King Charles, either, and beheaded him. When Henrietta's son Charles grew up, however, he seized back the English crown, and reinstalled his *maman* in her lavish London house.

CATHERINE OF ARAGON

1485–1536

MARRIED, BUT mostly confined to castle arrest for 27 years, Catherine of Aragon wrote tons of letters, including gooey ones to her husband, King Henry VIII. But when he commanded her to agree to his alliance with Anne Boleyn, she wrote to the pope, scorning Henry's tacky presumption:

"I came not into this realm as merchandise,
nor yet to be married to any merchant."

Poor Catherine had already been merchandised once, to Henry's tubercular brother Arthur, who died in her 17-year-old arms after four months of marriage. After she wed Henry, she did her queenly duty, producing seven babes, four of them the longed-for boys. All died early except little Mary. And so began Henry VIII's brutal, futile search for another womb—or five.

LUCREZIA BORGIA

1480–1519

BORN INTO the scandal-plagued Borgia clan, Lucrezia grew into a blonde bombshell. At 12, this graceful miss attended her first arranged marriage, to Giovanni Sforza, a glittering affair. But soon, a fatherly word, and *poof*!—marriage annulled on grounds of impotence.

Repurposed as virginal, Lucrezia wed another noble, who soon perished, falling victim to another Borgia specialty: assassin unknown.

After the demise of number two, the plucky pawn caught on. When Daddy pushed for remarriage, Lucrezia protested, saying:

". . . my husbands have been very unlucky."

Borgia bad luck was contagious, however. Lucrezia's philandering third husband gave her "the great pox," now called syphilis.

QUEEN CATHERINE PARR

1512–1548

"I am so vexed that I am utterly weary."

YOU'D BE weary too if you had to handle the puffy, petulant, wife-ditching Henry VIII for four long years.

After Henry VIII's funeral, his final wife got busy, finishing the controversial religious books she'd begun to write. Then the new widow lost her head, opting for true love—or so she thought. Thomas Seymour, Catherine's new spouse, speedily impregnated her, and then got busy hitting on young Elizabeth, the queen-to-be.

Parr died of childbed fever. Her demise was less grim than Seymour's end: involved in a conspiracy plot, he also lost his head—the literal, more painful way.

QUEEN ELIZABETH I

1533–1603

"When I think of marriage, it is as though my heart were being dragged out of my vitals."

If you had lived through what Elizabeth had by age 26, you'd be reluctant to legally link limbs with a male, too. Her father, after all, was the wife-disposing Henry VIII, who had condemned her mother, the spat-upon Anne Boleyn, to death by beheading. Elizabeth had also overcome treachery and religious plots launched by a scoundrel-filled court.

Elizabeth's role as the Virgin Queen suited her. Surrounded by adoring men seeking to entertain her with foreplay of the verbal sort, she always had first choice of dance partners. She could read whatever she liked and she got to make all the decisions. No wonder QE1 rose to the occasion for 45 years.

QUEEN CHRISTINA OF SWEDEN

1626–1689

GANGLY AND hump-shouldered, at home on a horse, good with guns, allergic to combs and dresses, Christina of Sweden shone at math, philosophy, and languages. After becoming queen, she brought the Renaissance to Sweden.

Seeking the next new thing, Christina abdicated in 1654, ditching Protestantism and her native land for Catholic Italy. The uproar didn't faze her:

"The news today threatens to engulf the world,
but I love the storm and fear the calm."

Now a filthy-rich civilian, Christina bounced around Europe, angling (without success) for another queendom. She left a trail of quotable quips, including one she epitomized:

"A person should aspire to be
an original, not a copy."

DOLLEY MADISON

1768–1849

WHEN JAMES MADISON became president in 1809, the nation gained a lively First Lady, fashionable and keen to decorate the new White House. Dolley's parties were can't-miss affairs—until the War of 1812 and the British capture of Washington in 1814. As the invading soldiers torched public buildings, most fled, but not Dolley. She stuck around to save art treasures and important papers. She later recollected:

"I confess that I was so unfeminine as to be free of fear, and willing to remain in the Castle. If I could have had a cannon through every window, but alas! Those who would have placed them there, had fled before me."

QUEEN EMMA OF HAWAII

1836–1885

IN MOURNING for her husband, King Liholiho, known as Kamehameha IV, who died only a year after their darling baby, Hawaii's Queen Emma was obliged to undergo a royal election. "Candidate Emma" was outraged at the idea that her lowlife opponent, Kalakaua, intended to sell off *her* islands.

The queen campaigned among her people, meanwhile declaring to the British:

> *"We have yet the right to dispose of our*
> *country as we wish, and be assured that it*
> *will never be to a Republic!"*

It took British *and* American troops to quell the riot after Emma's defeat.

SARAH JOSEPHA HALE
1788–1879

"If men cannot cope with women in the medical profession, let them take a humble occupation in which they can."

Witty and wise, this dynamo from New England was editor of *Godey's Lady's Book*, America's most popular magazine for decades. In an era without international copyright laws, American editors often lifted British articles for their periodicals. Sarah had unusual integrity; she paid writers $15 a page for their stories, and her mentorship encouraged the growth of American literature.

A prolific writer herself, Hale kicked out novels, nonfiction, women's history, and kiddie poetry. Her biggest hit? "Mary Had a Little Lamb," which became an early audio book of sorts: Edison recorded it to test his phonograph.

Besides influence, Sarah had gumption. She spent 17 years, lobbying five consecutive presidents, to make Thanksgiving a national holiday.

ANNIE BESANT

1847–1933

ANNIE BESANT married a man of God, but she found marriage to him hard going. Then she got behind the pulpit:

"I shall never forget the feeling of . . . delight
. . . as my voice rolled down the aisles."

ANNIE PROMPTLY abandoned her husband and threw herself into various isms, from atheism to socialism. Among her many writings was a fiery article entitled "The Legalization of Female Slavery in England."

Still seeking, Besant took up Theosophy and headed to India. After learning Sanskrit, translating sacred works, and starting a newspaper, Annie got nabbed by the British Raj and was imprisoned for activism. Unruffled, she emerged to become president of the Indian National Congress.

MARY ANN "MOTHER" BICKERDYKE

1817–1901

IN HER 40s, when her Union soldier son became gravely ill, Mary Ann Bickerdyke volunteered for battlefield aftercare. Dysentery and typhoid raged among the filth-covered wounded, and their care and feeding were abysmal.

Bickerdyke's skillful improvisation and amazing endurance saved thousands of desperate men. At times, this unpaid angel the men called "Mother" was the only nurse on the spot.

After the battle of Shiloh, a surgeon approached her, wondering aloud who she was and where she'd gotten the food, blankets, and coffee she dispensed. She retorted:

"I've received my authority from the
Lord God Almighty; you have anything
that ranks higher than that?"

Mother Bickerdyke personally marshaled cows, chickens, and other fresh resources from Chicago to feed and care for the wounded in the South. She set a new standard for getting things done.

MARY SURRATT

1823–1865

BEFORE THE Civil War, Mary Surratt owned slaves and a tobacco plantation; during the war, the widowed Mary opened a shabby boardinghouse in Washington, DC. As she struggled to survive, her son became tight pals with some fellow disgruntled Southerners, including an actor named John Booth. Their boardinghouse bull sessions got more intense, the men vowing "to act" if Lincoln became president again. Mary kept the conspirators and their secrets hidden.

One April night in 1865, detectives knocked on Surratt's door, demanding to search the house for Booth and Mary's son. Soon afterward, everyone at the boardinghouse was arrested for conspiracy. Surratt told her daughter:

"I think John Wilkes Booth was only an instrument in the hands of the Almighty to punish this proud and licentious people."

After her trial, an unrepentant Surratt went to the gallows, the first woman ever executed by the US government.

VICTORIA WOODHULL

1838–1927

A POLITICAL gadfly and the first female to run for US president, Victoria Woodhull made fortunes as a stockbroker and newspaper maven while grabbing headlines for her free-love stance. Despite her wild-child reputation, rumors that she had hornswoggled the millionaire Cornelius Vanderbilt, and her penchant for séances and other spiritual hokum, Woodhull believed in financial independence for women. This hardheaded feminist declared:

"Woman's ability to earn money is a better protection against the tyranny and brutality of man than her ability to vote."

QUEEN VICTORIA

1819–1901

A MONARCH whose rule over 250 million worldwide lasted 63 years, Queen Victoria wasn't as Victorian as history implies. At 16, she already had an eye for the lads. When her cousins Albert and Ernest visited, she cut loose, dancing to exhaustion with them and claiming:

"All this dissipation does me a great deal of good."

At 20, she proposed to Albert. As consort, he devoted himself to her, making the marriage bed a delight. The queen loathed pregnancies, however, and after baby number nine, her doctor forbade more. Victoria naively asked:

"Can I have no more fun in bed?"

It's hard to imagine what tips the doctor suggested, but she did have four more years—baby-free—to romp with Albert before his untimely death.

EMILIA BASSANO LANIER

1569–1645

THE 154 sizzling, sexy sonnets of Shakespeare were political-ly hot properties in 1609. Published without permission, they alluded to "the Dark Lady," thought by many to be luscious brunette Emilia Bassano Lanier. A talented poet, Emilia angri-ly skewered Will in return. In her 1611 book, she mocked Shakespeare's own lines, adding a well-turned diatribe against men behaving badly:

> *"Evil-disposed men forget that they were*
> *born of women, and nourished by women.*
> *. . . Men, like vipers, deface the wombs*
> *wherein they were bred."*

SARAH BERNHARDT

1844–1923

THE WORLD'S most famous stage actress in her day, and a pioneering silent-film star, Sarah Bernhardt was good copy. Besides her gorgeous face, the Divine Sarah flaunted a wooden limb after she lost her right leg when a stage injury led to amputation; at times she removed the prosthesis before performing.

An admirer gave Bernhardt a rosewood coffin, and it traveled everywhere with her. She would nap in it, often posing inside for photographers. When asked why she schlepped a casket, the Great One had a dramatic reply:

"My body will soon be dust [but]
my glory will live forever."

CHAPTER THREE

WARRIORS
FOR A RAINBOW
OF RIGHTS

EMILY *[surname unknown]*
1846–1863

ON CHATTANOOGA'S gore-spattered battlefield, a 17-year-old Union soldier lay dying. Earlier that year, she had proudly sent a daguerreotype image of herself in uniform to her family. On November 24, 1863, she dictated her faltering last words for a telegram home:

> *"Forgive your dying daughter. . . . My native soil drinks my blood. I expected to deliver my country but the fates would not have it so."*

In her final moments, she thought to add a postscript:

> *"P.S. Give my gold watch to little Eph."*

Trung Trac and Trung Nhi

CA. AD 12–CA. 43

WHEN THE sisters Trung Trac and Trung Nhi were born, Vietnam had been under China's thumb for centuries. In the year 39, the Chinese governor reminded the Vietnamese who was boss. After slaughtering her husband for daring to criticize, he raped Trung Trac.

Instead of becoming cowering victims, Trung Trac and her sister Nhi quietly rallied the Vietnamese. It took time. They trained leaders, many of them women, and organized 80,000 peasants. After expelling the hated governor, the sisters, riding elephants and waving sabers, led their freedom fighters to win 65 towns.

For three glorious years, Vietnam knew liberty. Eventually, however, the Chinese giant triumphed. The sisters chose to leave this world, committing ritual suicide in the river near their birthplace.

Each spring, at temples dedicated to the sisters across Vietnam, the words Trung Trac once spoke are still honored:

*"Foremost, I will avenge my country and
avenge the death of my husband."*

HARRIET TUBMAN

CA. 1821–1913

HAVING ESCAPED slavery at 25, Harriet Tubman refused to turn her back on others. As a conductor on the multistate Underground Railroad, she helped more than 300 slaves flee to Canada.

Harriet's own words upon reaching freedom were:

"When I found I had crossed that line, I looked at my hands to see if I was the same person. There was such a glory over everything; the sun came like gold through the trees, and over the fields, and I felt like I was in Heaven."

ABIGAIL GRANT

ACTIVE 1776

COLONIAL WOMEN settled the American wilderness, handled firearms, and did it all without indoor plumbing or much help while their men were busy fighting the British.

When pioneer Abigail Grant got word of her husband's less-than-heroic war record, she fired a stinging reply, which included this excerpt:

"I hear by Capt. Wm. Riley news that makes me very Sorry for he Says you proved a Grand Coward when the fight was at Bunkers hill. . . . If you are afraid pray own the truth & come home & take care of our Children & I will be Glad to Come & take your place."

SARAH OSBORN BENJAMIN

CA. 1750–1837

GEORGE WASHINGTON had unsung female assets in his Continental Army: camp followers, who made the hellish lives of soldiers a bit better. As his army trudged through the snow to recapture Philadelphia, a private's wife named Sarah drew Washington's eye. Before battles, she routinely carried beef, bread, and coffee to the men in the trenches.

Washington asked her, "Aren't you afraid of the cannonballs?"

Sarah commonsensically replied:

"It would not do for the men
to fight and starve too."

MARY HOOKS SLOCUMB

1760–1836

DURING THE Revolutionary War, teenage Mary Hooks Slocumb woke from a bloody nightmare about her husband, a troop commander. Sick with dread, she galloped her mare 40 miles to the battlefield. With pressure bandages and herbal remedies, she circulated among the wounded, fighting blood loss while searching for him. Spotting a family friend who had taken bullets to thigh and head, she rendered aid.

When her husband appeared, he joked, "Why, Mary, what are you doing here? Hugging Frank, the biggest reprobate in the army?"

Mary bantered back, joyous that her husband was alive. Her diary entry that evening says it all:

"I was so happy—and so were all!
It was a glorious victory."

ELIZABETH "MUM BETT" FREEMAN

CA. 1742–1829

THE SHINY new Declaration of Independence got Elizabeth Freeman, a much-abused slave known as Mum Bett, to thinking. Fleeing to find her own liberty, she encountered an abolition-minded advocate, Theodore Sedgwick, who argued before a Massachusetts court for her freedom in 1781.

The result was joyous: the jury found for her! After celebrating, Mum Bett worked for her attorney's family as governess to the Sedgwick children.

Freeman's case had far-reaching implications: it ended slavery in Massachusetts, and gave other states (and slaves) hope.

Catharine, a Sedgwick child who became an author, gave permanent form to Mum Bett's eloquent words:

"While I was a slave, if one minute's freedom had been offered to me, and I'd been told I must die at the end of that minute, I would have taken it—just to stand one minute on God's earth a free woman."

ELENA DE CÉSPEDES

CA. 1545–CA. 1588

BORN A Moorish slave, by 16 Elena had been impregnated, wed, and abandoned. She longed for a more rewarding life, a future like what men had, for instance, so Elena began a lifelong transition to Eleno. De Céspedes served five years in the military, worked as a tailor, then studied medicine and became a barber-surgeon, all the while perfecting a masculine identity. When Eleno fell in love and wanted to wed a young woman, neighbors denounced the couple and de Céspedes was put on trial for sodomy and sorcery, telling the Inquisition judges:

> *"In reality, I am and I was a hermaphrodite.*
> *I have and had two natures, one a man*
> *and another, a woman."*

When her examiners found no male genitalia, de Céspedes explained that she was born a woman, but popped out a male appendage when giving birth. Years later, after an injury on horseback, Dr. Eleno had to perform a do-it-yourself amputation of this post-pregnancy appendage. While this tale may sound implausible to us, it nicely fit the ancient medical theories the Spaniards believed.

De Céspedes's slave-to-surgeon saga and learned defense won over her inquisitors. Well, partially. The defendant was still found guilty but escaped being burned at the stake. After a 200-lash public whipping, de Céspedes was sentenced to treat patients at a charity hospital. For 10 years. As Elena. In female garb.

Spaniards had avidly followed the trial and soon overran the hospital, eager to be seen by this miraculously self-made person, whatever the gender.

Frances E. W. Harper
1825–1911

AFRICAN AMERICAN author Frances Harper made abolition speeches in her home state of Maryland and was one of the compassionate thousands who helped runaway slaves gain freedom.

"I send you to-day two dollars for the Underground Rail Road. It is only a part of what I subscribed at your meeting. . . . I am still in the lecturing field. . . . Send me word what I can do for the fugitive."

HARRIET BEECHER STOWE

1811–1896

BITTER LAUDANUM, a liquid tincture of opium alkaloids, became the painkiller of choice for young and old in the 19th century. Author Harriet Beecher Stowe knew its potency. She used it to powerful effect in her novel *Uncle Tom's Cabin*:

"Whipping and abuse are like laudanum; you have to double the dose as the sensibilities decline."

Her novel struck a nerve, polarizing people and jump-starting the Civil War. More than 305,000 copies were sold in 1852, the year the book came out.

MARY ELIZABETH BOWSER

BORN CA. 1839

WHEN THE American Civil War began, Mary Elizabeth Bowser (a former slave freed and educated by her former owner, Elizabeth Van Lew) went undercover to help the Union side. After scoring a menial job at Confederate headquarters in Jefferson Davis's home, Bowser, while playing a simple, illiterate servant, adroitly memorized documents and eavesdropped on conversations, later repeating everything to Van Lew. Transcriptions of her invaluable data, hidden in shoes and food items, went straight to army higher-ups.

Near war's end, Confederates suspected spies in their midst but never pinpointed Bowser.

Despite her courage, Mary found the postwar period very troubling. She taught, lectured, and changed identities, but her dismay shows in this passage:

"I wish there was some law here, or some protection. I know the southerners pretty well ... having been in the service so long as a detective that I still find myself scrutinizing them closely. ... Do not ... laugh at my letter. Anyone that has spent 4 months in Richmond prison does not be so easily frightened."

SARAH GRIMKÉ

1792–1873

BORN INTO a South Carolina slave-holding family, Sarah Grimké saw a slave savagely beaten when she was a child. She fled the scene, horrified.

Unsurprisingly, as an adult Grimké waded into the abolitionist movement. Known for her antislavery tracts, this confirmed feminist, who declined to marry, also defended women's rights with crackling good prose:

"I ask no favors for my sex. All I ask of our brethren is, that they will take their feet from off our necks, and permit us to stand upright on that ground which God designed us to occupy."

Her courageous convictions rattled windows and ultimately hearts.

SOJOURNER TRUTH

1799–1883

SIX-FOOT-TALL Isabella Baumfree, unafraid to be outrageous, renamed herself Sojourner Truth. The first thing she did when given liberty in 1827 was sue a rich white man who had sold her son into slavery in Alabama.

Her deep voice cast a spell over any audience. A tireless speaker, she met the challenges raised by hecklers head-on. In Indiana once, when accused of being a male, Sojourner bared her breast to the audience, adding:

> *"And I've suckled many a white babe,*
> *to the exclusion of my own."*

ANGELINA GRIMKÉ

1805–1879

THE YOUNGER of the two reform-minded Grimké sisters, Angelina had dynamic lecturing skills. She and her sister, Sarah, both ignored those who frowned on Southern women speaking publicly.

Men as well as women crowded in to hear Angelina when the sisters toured New England. In 1838, after she and Sarah submitted antislavery petitions to Massachusetts's legislators, Angelina gleefully remarked:

"We abolition women are turning the world upside down."

After emancipation, when Angelina was in her 60s, she braved a snowstorm to go out with her sister and 42 other women. It was election day, and the Grimké pioneers and friends wanted to vote.

ELIZABETH HOBBS KECKLEY

1818–1907

"No common mortal has died—
the Moses of my people has fallen."

That cry came from dressmaker Elizabeth Keckley upon viewing the body of Abraham Lincoln. She had special reasons to mourn; she had become the friend and confidante of the fallen president's wife, Mary Todd Lincoln.

An abused slave who had worked hard to buy her own freedom at 37 and to become an author, Keckley founded a relief group, in Abe's honor, to help former slaves make the transition that she had made.

MARIA WESTON CHAPMAN
1806–1885

"How heretical, harsh, fanatical,
moon-struck, unsexed I am."

Abolitionist Maria Weston Chapman wrote those words to a friend when she was having misgivings about her activism. Most who knew of her, however, admired her energy and considered her a fantastic fund-raiser. One of her best ideas was holding antislavery fairs, where handiwork with clever messages was sold. Pen wipers bore the logo "Wipe out the blot of slavery," while linens were embroidered "May our needles prick the slaveholders' consciences."

HELEN HUNT JACKSON
1830–1885

"If I could write a story that would do for the Indian a thousandth part what Uncle Tom's Cabin did for the Negro, I would be thankful the rest of my life."

Author Helen Hunt Jackson gave it her best shot. *Ramona*, her novel about the mistreatment of Native Americans, sold faster than a California wildfire. It became a classic, though not the shocking eye-opener that *Cabin* had been.

After hearing Chief Standing Bear describe the removal of his Ponca tribe of Nebraska to Oklahoma territory, Jackson got more political. She wrote *A Century of Dishonor*, a sharp indictment of governmental brutality toward tribal cultures after the Mexican-American War. To put her accusations in front of the guilty parties, Jackson sent personalized copies to every member of Congress.

SARAH WINNEMUCCA

CA. 1844–1891

"I've never seen a president . . . and I want to know whether he is made of wood or rock. . . . No human would send people across a fearful mountain in mid-winter."

A member of the Piutes of the American West, Sarah Winnemucca should be more famous than Pocahontas, given her extraordinary efforts to bring about interracial understanding. At Winnemucca's birth, Piute lands stretched from Nevada into Oregon. As her tribe was pushed from one reservation to another, Sarah became its fearless spokesperson.

After chiding President Rutherford B. Hayes, Sarah went on lecture tours that took her from California to the East Coast to publicize her people's plight. She wrote *Life among the Piutes*, the first book in English by a Native American woman. It cleverly contained a mail-in petition to lobby Congress.

The ruckus Winnemucca created won federal promises; tragically, all were broken. Sarah returned to teaching, founding a school for Indian children and working there until tuberculosis stole her life at age 48.

CLARA BARTON

1821–1912

A TOP-NOTCH organizer; a woman who tended the Civil War's injured midbattle, her long skirts becoming heavy with blood; and a tireless healer who thought of the fighting men as "her boys"—that was Clara Barton.

After the Civil War, Barton had a nervous breakdown. Boredom, she said. To heal, Barton volunteered in Europe. Impressed with the International Red Cross, she returned to jump-start the American Red Cross.

Unable to sit still, Barton later focused on voting rights. She made a pitch to all the vets she had helped:

> *"When you were weak and I was strong,*
> *I toiled for you. Now you are strong . . .*
> *and I ask your aid . . . for the ballot."*

MARY HARRIS "MOTHER" JONES

1837–1930

SHE HAD survived the Irish potato famine and a yellow fever epidemic that wiped out her entire family. Now, after losing her dressmaking business in the Great Chicago Fire of 1871, Mary Jones headed for the labor hall to get help.

This 40-something had no inkling she would spend the next 50-something years helping miners, tackling child labor, and harassing odious business owners such as John D. Rockefeller Jr.

The one issue Mother Jones, as she became known, never spent time on was suffrage for women—she called it a diversion. In countless speeches, she hollered:

> *"You don't need a vote to raise hell!*
> *You need convictions and a voice!"*

MARY ELIZABETH LEASE

1850–1933

AFTER MARY Elizabeth Lease and her spouse lost their Kansas farm in the Panic of 1874, they moved to Texas, where Mary studied law. Then she lost her heart to politics. Lease became notorious for the slogan she shouted to farmers:

"Raise less corn and more hell!"

It turns out that reporters had coined the phrase first. Other Lease quotes, however, sound relevant even today:

"Wall Street owns the country. It is no longer a government of the people, by the people, and for the people, but a government of Wall Street, by Wall Street, and for Wall Street."

CARRIE NATION

1846–1911

"Men, I have come to save you
from a drunkard's fate!"

A main driver of the temperance movement before Prohibition even existed, Carrie Nation was a Kentucky bulldog who began her campaign after her husband hit the bottle.

First she cruised taverns, calling bartenders "destroyers of men's souls." Gradually, Nation got a more grandiose, multistate vision. Carrying rocks and waving a hatchet, she created havoc while singing hymns in the bars of Kansas, Missouri, and other states.

Routinely arrested for these acts, called "hatchetations," Nation paid jail fines out of her lecture fees, a perk of her growing notoriety. (Nation also sold a nice line of souvenir hatchets and "home defender" pins.)

To some she became a figure of fun, but Carrie continued her dead-serious fight, even preaching her no-booze message in vaudeville venues. Only her own mortality brought Nation to a halt.

IDA WELLS-BARNETT

1862–1931

THE HEINOUS vigilante act of lynching became ominously frequent after the Civil War. In 1892 alone, violence against blacks included 235 lynchings.

A gutsy African American schoolteacher and journalist named Ida Wells took it upon herself to wake Americans up, and to rally her Memphis community. Her hard-hitting journalism in the 1880s named names and described lynchings without euphemism.

Published despite death threats, her brave voice generated national awareness and action. When three Memphis grocery-store owners were lynched, she advised blacks to leave the city; some 6,000 did.

After marrying and moving to Chicago, Ida Wells-Barnett continued to fight racism and write about lynching in national and European publications.

Her tombstone reads:

*"She told the truth in words so stirring
that she forced the world to listen."*

CHAPTER FOUR

UNFETTERED IS BETTER

MARY EDMONIA LEWIS

1844–1907

WILDFIRE WAS her Ojibwa name. Orphaned early, this bright child of African American and Native American heritage went to college at 15, subsidized by her brother's gold-rush success. To fit in, she renamed herself Mary Edmonia Lewis.

But she didn't fit in. After she made spiced wine for her roommates, they fell deathly ill. Accusations of poisoning—and worse—flew. The girls recovered, but some townspeople waylaid Lewis one evening and beat her severely. In a bizarre, racially motivated twist, *she* was arrested, not the attackers. The ugly affair went to trial. A jury found her innocent, but this individual had had enough.

Lewis chose a new life path, as a sculptor in Boston. By selling her work, she financed a trip to Rome. She found Italy less race-conscious, and made it her new home. Wildfire created large-scale marble sculptures that won acclaim, some with Native American themes. About her artistic destiny, she mused:

"How strange [that] the Great Spirit has led me on without father or mother."

SARAH EMMA EDMONDS

1842–1898

A CANADIAN runaway, Sara dressed as a boy and sold Bibles door to door. During the Civil War, calling herself Franklin Thompson, she joined a Michigan regiment and fought on the Union side for years.

She had several hairy assignments, first as spy, then as mail carrier, fording swift streams on horseback. But Edmonds's favorite duty was hospital work, until malarial fever led her to desert, fearing exposure. Nevertheless, she managed to return to the battlefront with a civilian contingent, this time as a female nurse.

After the war, Sarah penned a quasi-factual page-turner of her adventures, which sold more than 175,000 copies. In *Nurse and Spy in the Union Army*, the gender-agile Sarah/Frank gave this motive for enlisting:

"I went to war with no other ambition than to nurse the sick and care for the wounded."

MARIE LE JARS DE GOURNAY

1565–1645

*"Men and women are equal in everything
—except opportunity."*

That acerbic remark came from a French mademoiselle who made her own opportunities. Self-taught, an able translator, and a bold believer in asking, she wrote fan letters to the big celebrity of her day, essayist Michel de Montaigne. They corresponded, gradually becoming good friends.

After his death in 1609, Michel's widow asked Marie to edit his essays. The prestige of this assignment led to ghost writing for a host of royals, which led to actual pay. She also got a royal go-ahead to publish six of her own works. When not writing, de Gournay dabbled in alchemy. She stayed single for nearly 80 years, and preferred it that way, as she affirmed:

*"I want no husband other than honor,
enriched by the reading of good books."*

CAROLINE HERSCHEL

1750–1848

CAROLINE WAS William Herschel's little sister in more ways than one: she'd stopped growing after childhood typhus. There was nothing wrong with her brain, though. When her big brother went mad for astronomy, the heavens likewise became Caroline's lifework. At times, she surpassed him.

This German gem could hand-grind mirrors for telescopes as well as she could run laborious calculations. In her 30s, she made her own studies with a 27-inch Newtonian scope. Within five years, she had discovered eight comets and three nebulae.

Caroline's biggest shock? She became the first woman to get any dough for her science contributions. In her memoirs, she recalled the thrill:

"It was the first money in all my lifetime
. . . to spend to my liking."

The stargazing doyenne lived to age 97; late in life she admitted:

"I'm now so accustomed to receiving honors, that I
take them . . . without blushing."

LADY TRIEU

CA. 228–248

IN THE centuries-long tug-of-war between China and its neighbor Vietnam, resistance in the latter land sometimes came from a surprising direction: female freedom fighters. Once it came from a teen who called herself Lady Trieu.

Motivated by an earlier Vietnamese rebellion led by the Trung sisters, she decided to emulate them. Her brother protested, suggesting she stick to conventional behavior. Before her suicide mission, the defiant 19-year-old gave a spirited answer:

"I want to ride the tempest, tame the waves, kill the sharks. I will not resign myself to the usual lot of women who bow their heads and become housewives. Or concubines."

LORETA JANETA VELÁZQUEZ

1842–CA. 1902

THE AMERICAN Civil War was a young man's—and often a young woman's—fight. One of hundreds of daring dames who passed themselves off as male was Cuban-born Loreta Velázquez, who signed up with the Confederate forces as Harry T. Buford.

Wearing a man's wig, a large mustache, and a beard, she smoked cigars in macho fashion. As a lieutenant, she side-stepped duties that might have given her away, as she notes in a surviving letter:

"There are some things which men can do better than women, and digging [ditches] in frozen ground is one of them . . . nature had evidently intended me for a warrior rather than a dirt-digger."

Eleanor of Aquitaine

CA. 1122–1204

BESIDES REIGNING as France's queen for 15 years and England's queen for several decades, feisty Eleanor of Aquitaine spent years in prison.

In her 60s, when she emerged from house arrest, she decided to do something for England's nonroyal jailbirds. She declared an amnesty, releasing all captives:

> *"I have learned by experience that imprisonment is distasteful to mankind and it is a most delightful refreshment to the spirits to be liberated therefrom."*

There was one caveat: the newly freed had to peacefully support the new government—meaning Eleanor and son Richard the Lionheart.

PERPETUA OF CARTHAGE

CA. 178–203

PERPETUA SHOCKED her Roman parents when she rebelled and became a Christian activist in Carthage, Tunisia. Soon she and members of her group were imprisoned for proselytizing. After their appearance before a magistrate, Perpetua wrote in her diary:

> *"Hilarianus passed sentence on all of us; we were condemned to the beasts, and we returned to prison in high spirits."*

The arena date arrived; Perpetua handed off her diary to an eye-witness. Her male comrades got mauled by carnivores. When Perpetua's turn came, a wild heifer tossed her. Largely uninjured, she shouted:

> *"You must . . . not be weakened by what we have gone through."*

All the martyrs received a final sword thrust into the neck. When the gladiator got to Perpetua, he missed, hitting bone. The eyewitness wrote:

"She took the trembling hand of the
gladiator and guided it to her throat. It was
as though . . . she could not be dispatched
unless she herself were willing."

THÉRÈSE OF LISIEUX

1873–1897

A FRENCH Carmelite nun known as the Little Flower and declared a saint for her simple holiness, Thérèse of Lisieux wrote an openhearted autobiography that remains a treasure. Her sunny precepts have never been improved upon.

"You ask me for a method of attaining perfection.
I know Love—and Love only! Our hearts
are made for it alone."

MARTHA TUNSTALL SMITH

ACTIVE 1707

WHEN HER colonel husband, a landlubber, expired, Martha Tunstall (sometimes spelled Turnstall) Smith chose a career after her own heart: whaling. Despite the odious and odoriferous nature of this enterprise, this Long Island widow dived in. Her logbook shows exactly how hands-on Martha was:

"Feb. ye 4, 1707. Indian Harry . . . struck a stunt whale and could not kill it—called for my boat to help him."

"Feb., ye 22, 1707. My two boats, and my son's, and Floyd's boats, killed a yearling whale, of which I had half."

GRACE BEDELL

1848–1936

LINCOLN OCCASIONALLY answered his own mail. In 1860, he responded to 11-year-old New Yorker Grace Bedell's request—and obeyed it.

"I . . . want you should be President of the United States very much . . . I have got 4 brothers and part of them will vote for you any way and if you will let your whiskers grow I will try and get the rest of them to vote for you . . . you would look a great deal better for your face is so thin. All the ladies like whiskers and they would tease their husbands to vote for you."

JOANNA SOUTHCOTT

1750–1814

CENTURIES BEFORE the Internet, British visionary Joanna Southcott pumped out prophecies, some actually realized, and soon gained more than 100,000 believers.

At age 64, the spinster-prophetess claimed to have received the following marriage proposal from the spirit world:

"Order twelve gowns for thy wedding."

Not long after her wedding announcement, Southcott told followers she was pregnant with God's child, Shiloh. As she grew in girth, 21 doctors verified Joanna's pregnancy, sending sales of her talismans through the roof. Although Joanna's beliefs were genuine, her interesting condition wasn't; she died as deflated as her groupies.

JUANA INÉS DE LA CRUZ

1651–1695

A BOOKWORM at three, Juana Inés de la Cruz adored her grandfather's library. Recognizing her lively mind, others paid for her education. As a teen she entered convent life; besides undertaking her religious duties, Juana assembled the largest collection of books and scientific instruments ever seen in Mexico.

She also composed powerful poetry, including love lyrics addressed to women and men. As time went on, the nun's daring mix of religious and worldly themes made some uneasy. An angry bishop attacked her work, calling it "audacious" and "inappropriate." Even worse, their debate went public. Her eloquent answer included this excerpt:

> *"I became a nun . . . given the total disinclination*
> *I felt toward marriage, it seemed the most*
> *fitting and decent thing I could do."*

Distraught that she wasn't sufficiently pious, Juana sold her library and donated the proceeds to the poor. When plague struck Mexico City, this spirited woman hit the streets, nursing the sick and dying, until she too succumbed.

Manuela Sáenz

1797–1856

An Ecuadorian beauty, afire with revolutionary enthusiasm, Manuela Sáenz caught the eye of continent-conquering hero Simón Bolívar in 1822. Although he maintained a lineup of mistresses, Manuela became his favorite.

She helped him escape assassination, and the two cohabited until his death, notwithstanding a previous commitment to her rich husband. As she deftly redefined it:

"Marriage pledges one to nothing."

PAULINE BONAPARTE

1780–1825

NAPOLEON I GRABBED the glory, but other Bonapartes were also tabloid-worthy. The emperor's unfettered sister Pauline was noted for gorgeousness and binge spending on jewels. Pauline bedded numerous men, until a grotesquely endowed painter gave her what doctors quaintly called "womb exhaustion."

This uninhibited coquette also posed for a now-famous Venus sculpture by Antonio Canova. When prissy friends huffed about her buff state, she shrugged and said:

"It wasn't cold. There was a fire in the studio."

DOROTHY LEVITT

1882–1922

WHEN ADMIRERS called her the "fastest girl on earth," they weren't referring to her sex life. Dorothy Levitt came out of nowhere to race the earliest speedboats and cars, setting records with both. Levitt had turned passionate about driving when a friend stopped by with a newfangled motorcar. That instant, she became a dashing female at the wheel.

England's speed demoness once took a pit stop to write a jolly-sounding advice tome, *The Woman and the Car: A Chatty Little Handbook for All Women Who Motor or Who Want to Motor.* Levitt readily confessed:

"I prefer steering a really fast motorcar to anything else in the world."

VIOLANTE DO CÉU

CA. 1601-1693

AN ARISTOCRAT who swanned into a Portuguese convent in her 20s, Violante do Céu had written poetry since she was a girl. Within the convent walls, inspiration struck, and she penned, among many other poems, one entitled:

"Voice of a Dissipated Woman inside a Tomb, Talking to Another Woman Who Presumed to Enter Church with the Purpose of Being Seen and Praised by Everyone, Who Sat Down near a Sepulchre Containing This Epitaph, Which Curiously Reads."

Violante may have created a new poetic form, in which the title did all the work. It's hard to believe it never caught on, isn't it?

EMILY DICKINSON
1830–1886

EMILY DICKINSON'S father often purchased new reading material for her, and then forbade her to look inside. As Emily put it:

> *"He buys me many Books—but begs*
> *me not to read them—because he*
> *fears they joggle the Mind."*

Emily proved her brain was safe from ill effects of joggling. Deftly evading marriage and childbearing, housebound by choice, she let her mind soar, living a quietly adventurous and creative life. At her death, her astounded family found 1,700 poems she had written, now considered gems of American literature.

ROSA BONHEUR

1822–1899

AN ARTIST'S daughter, Rosa came by her talent and eccentricity naturally. Painting animals became her forte. Her hobbies revolved around cigarettes and female companionship. Her animal art also benefited from her longtime relationship with a woman who was an amateur veterinarian.

Once teased for socializing at a males-only gathering without a chaperone, Bonheur commented drily:

"If you knew how little I care for your sex, you wouldn't get any ideas. In the way of males, I like only the bulls I paint."

JULIANA BERNERS

CA. 1430–1490

PRIORESS OF a nunnery in Saint Albans, England, Juliana Berners came from a highfalutin family, but her true passions were outdoor pursuits, from falconry to fishing. An early environmentalist, Berners understood the implications of over-fishing. In the first book ever published on fly-fishing, which many believe to have been written by Berners, the author noted:

"You must not be too greedy in catching your said game, as in taking too much at one time, a thing which can easily happen."

Susan B. Anthony

1820–1906

A BARE-KNUCKLED fighter for equal wages and the right to vote, Susan B. Anthony was arrested and fined $100 for trying to cast her ballot in 1872. She refused to pay. Ever defiant, Anthony also challenged the sanctity of the wedded state:

"Marriage, to women as to men, must be a luxury, not a necessity; an incident of life, not all of it. And the only possible way to accomplish this great change is to accord to women equal power."

IDA LEWIS

1842–1911

RARELY WERE women appointed lighthouse keepers, but Ida Lewis had ideal qualifications. Besides being handy with oil-lamp beacons, she made a habit of daring rescues during the 39 years she lived on Rhode Island's Lime Rock.

At 17, Lewis fished four guys out of the drink when their sailboat capsized. In 1869, she rescued two waterlogged soldiers during a snowstorm. The year Lewis turned 63, a friend lost her balance and fell overboard while rowing out to see her. Lewis pulled her to safety.

The first woman given the US Coast Guard's prestigious Gold Lifesaving Medal, Ida Lewis became a household name, raved about in the press as the "Bravest Woman in America" and visited by President Ulysses S. Grant. After each lifesaving drama, reporters hounded her for more stories, more quotes. Instead, Ida repeated what she had said after her very first rescue:

*"I did not think the matter worth talking about,
and never gave it a second thought."*

HYPATIA OF ALEXANDRIA

CA. 355–415

THE GREEK mathematician Hypatia, who taught astronomy and philosophy in ancient Alexandria, had a huge fan base and devoted students, as well as admirers wanting to marry her. A diplomat as well as a philosopher, Hypatia allegedly turned down her suitors by gently saying:

"I'm wedded to the truth."

This intellectual lived in dangerous times, when leaders locked horns over Christianity, Judaism, and polytheism. A high-profile pagan, Hypatia made a tempting target for extremists. One day, fanatics dragged her into a church, stripped her, and cut her naked body into pieces. None of the assassins was wedded to the truth, evidently. No one ever stood trial.

LOUISA MAY ALCOTT

1832–1888

SOON REALIZING her dad was a dud at bringing home the bacon, Louisa May Alcott became the financial mainstay of her intellectually progressive family. When a publisher asked her to write a book for girls, Alcott initially dumped on the idea, saying:

> *"Never liked girls or knew*
> *many, except my sisters."*

Nevertheless, she complied, and *Little Women* became a surprise best seller, and Alcott had the good sense to retain copyright. Her output grew to 29 books, and her work, including lurid short stories written under pseudonyms, appeared in myriad collections.

Alcott never married, saying she had never had romantic feelings for a man. A committed feminist with a large circle of friends, she lived a philosophy she had coined:

> *"Liberty is a better husband than*
> *love to many of us."*

CHAPTER FIVE

SOUL MATES AND ODD COUPLES

FLORENCE NIGHTINGALE
AND MARY SEACOLE
1820–1910 • 1805–1881

THE CRIMEAN War didn't stand a chance when two irascible fireballs of nursing savvy headed its way. In short order, Florence Nightingale healed the wounded, did what she could for the cholera-ridden, and trained platoons of nurses. An 1860 statement reveals her frustration about how her profession was perceived:

> *"Not even a doctor . . . gives any other definition of what a nurse should be than . . . 'devoted and obedient.' . . . This definition might even do for a horse."*

Mary Seacole, nicknamed "the black Nightingale," set up a recuperation facility for officers and grunts behind the lines. A traditional Jamaican healer, Mary also understood how contagious diseases were spread. Nursing stints in the West Indies during epidemics gave her invaluable experience, to the benefit of the soldiers suffering in Crimea. Seacole's request to serve had been rejected, but she went to Crimea anyway, as she recounted in 1853:

"I made up my mind that if the army wanted nurses, they would be glad of me. . . . I would go to the Crimea; and go I did, as all the world knows."

KATHARINA VON BORA

1499–1552

MARTIN LUTHER helped liberate a group of nuns from a German convent by smuggling them out in herring barrels. One of them, Katharina von Bora, took a shine to her Protestant hero. The pair married, and theirs became a loving partnership. Stalwart Katie planted fields, gave birth to six Luther children, fed 40 boarders, and made darned good beer.

After Martin's death, she continued to cope but had to flee invading armies and the Black Plague. Her last words were said to be:

"I will stick to Christ as a burr to a topcoat."

DIDYMA AND ISADORA OF EGYPT

1ST CENTURY BC

IN PRIOR millennia, women routinely hired others to suckle newborns. Fascinating proof has been found amid mummy wrappings in Egypt: a 2,000-year-old papyrus contract signed by two women—Isadora, who had found an abandoned baby and kept it to raise as a slave, and Didyma, hired to care for and feed the child. The 16-month contract was very specific:

> *"Didyma agrees to nurse and suckle . . .*
> *at her own home . . . with her own*
> *milk, pure and untainted."*

Didyma further agreed not to sleep with any men, and to bring the child for weekly inspection. As wet nurse, she received 12 silver drachmas and a half-liter of oil monthly. Isadora had to keep her side of the bargain, too: she risked stiff penalties for noncompliance, including a 500-drachma fine.

MARIE-MADELEINE DE MONTREUIL

ACTIVE MID-1700S

AFTER MARRYING off her oldest daughter, Renée, proto-tiger mother Marie-Madeleine de Montreuil sighed with relief. Donatien de Sade was a charming, witty son-in-law; there were rumors of orgies and whip-fests, but he made Renée happy.

Before long, though, de Sade's scandals and debts began to mount. The final straw? The marquis seduced Madame Marie's convent-pure youngest. In a fury, Marie-Madeleine obtained a formidable weapon, a *lettre de cachet*, signed by the king, ordering her son-in-law's arrest without trial. With that she got the sodomy-happy aristocrat thrown into prison. Madame exulted:

"All is now in order."

With de Sade's pattern of escape and recapture, however, having him permanently imprisoned became Madame Enforcer's life-work. While he wrote book-length, XXX-rated rants during one 13-year lockup, still-adoring Renée brought him favorite foods and even sexy toys. But at last, Marie-Madeleine persuaded her clueless daughter to divorce the marquis de Sade. He would spend his final decade in an insane asylum.

ANNIE OAKLEY

1860–1926

OHIO-BORN Annie Oakley often skipped school in order to hunt game to support her family. When a sharpshooting act hit Cincinnati, the intrepid teen competed against its star, Frank Butler. He lost the $100 bet he had placed—but won Oakley's heart. The couple, hitched within a year, joined Buffalo Bill's Wild West troupe; fellow performer Sitting Bull nicknamed her "Little Sure Shot."

The company triumphantly toured Europe, and the petite superstar impressed Queen Victoria and other elites. In 1898, conscientious and concerned about the looming Spanish-American War, Oakley wrote to President William McKinley:

> *"I for one feel Confident that your good*
> *judgment will carry America safely through*
> *without war—but in case of such an event*
> *I am ready to place a Company of fifty*
> *Lady sharpshooters at your disposal."*

His "no, thanks" was one of the few refusals charming Annie ever got.

WIBRANDIS ROSENBLATT

1504–1564

AN OSTENSIBLY sensible Swiss, Wibrandis Rosenblatt habitually married church reformers, three of them—all poor, often sent into exile, and prone to getting plague. Was Rosenblatt a candidate for sainthood or a woman with a martyr complex? History judges her an important background figure in the Protestant Reformation movement. Yet a letter to her theology student son at a German university offers clues that she did not find her role as helpmeet and mother a comfortable one:

"I haven't heard from you in some time, but I well know that if I had, the news would not have been comforting. You contrive always to be a cross to me. If only I might live to the day when I have good news from you. Then I would die of joy."

FURIA SPES

ACTIVE AD 100

ROMAN WOMEN, even of modest means, remembered their loved ones with eloquent memorials. Furia Spes, a former slave, left this testimonial:

"Furia Spes, freedwoman . . . provided this memorial for her dearly beloved husband. When we were still boy and girl, we were bound by mutual love as soon as we met. . . . We were separated by a cruel hand when we should have continued to live in happiness. I therefore beg, most sacred manes *[spirits of the dead], that you look after the loved one I have entrusted to you and that you be . . . very kind to him during the hours of the night, so that I may see him [in dreams] and so that he, too, may . . . allow me to come to him, softly and soon."*

SUSETTE AND SUSAN LA FLESCHE

1854–1903 • 1865–1915

DAUGHTERS OF Omaha tribal chief Joseph La Flesche, Susette and Susan attended the best schools their father could afford. Their goals were to address the desperate challenges faced by their fellow Native Americans. Susan, the first female medical school graduate of her people, spoke with devastating honesty:

"We who are educated have to be pioneers of Indian civilization. We have to prepare our people to live in the white man's way, to use the white man's books, and to use his laws if you will only give them to us."

Her teacher sister Susette became a hard-core rights advocate, protesting lustily to the Indian Affairs commissioner:

"It's all a farce when you say you're trying to civilize us, then, after we educate ourselves, refuse us positions of responsibility and leave us utterly powerless to help ourselves. Perhaps the only way to make ourselves heard is to appeal to the American public through the press. They might listen."

LI CH'ING CHAO

1084–1151

WHAT'S RARER than a love match in medieval China? Two culture-mad scholars whose loving memories still persist.

For 25 years, Li Ch'ing Chao and her husband, Chao Ming-Ch'eng, lived a dream, rich in affection and cultural treasures. Ignoring poverty, Li extolled their happy-go-lucky times:

"Chao would pawn one of his robes . . .
then buy rubbings and books plus fruit and nuts.
. . . The two of us would open the books, admire the
rubbings, and exchange remarks of appreciation
while munching the food, calling ourselves
citizens of the utopian period."

The couple became refugees when their Chinese city fell to Jurchen tribes during the Jin–Song Wars. Chao died; Li honored him by publishing his manuscript on antiques. Ten centuries on, she's still revered as a scholar and poet.

Jessie Benton Frémont

1824–1902

JESSIE FRÉMONT had a vivid way with words. Missouri senator Thomas Hart Benton's daughter, she married future California senator John C. Frémont. Jessie turned her husband's plodding prose about his explorations of the Far West and California into poetry. Her vivacious personality also wowed crowds when John ran for (and lost) the presidency in 1856.

Although an excellent explorer, John was as deplorable at finances as he was at writing. Throughout their marriage, Jessie was the gallant vessel, keeping the family above water. She apparently liked the challenge, proclaiming:

"I am like a deeply built ship—I drive best under a strong wind."

MARY TATTLE-WELL AND JOANE HIT-HIM-HOME, SPINSTERS

ACTIVE 1640

FOUR DECADES after the death of good Queen Bess, England was on its way to civil war, and the monarchy, Parliament, and citizens were in turmoil. Women activists took to the streets to advocate for workers' rights, and grabbed quill pens to snipe about the mistreatment of housewives.

One merry example was *The Womens Sharpe Revenge*, which appeared with the byline "Mary Tattle-Well and Joane Hit-Him-Home, Spinsters." The authors argued against trade restrictions and the overemphasis on marriage as the best avenue for females.

"If thou beest of the Masculine Sexe, we meane thee and thee only . . . yet suffer you us to be reviled, and railed at, taunted & terrified, undervalu'd, and even vilified, when among you all Wee cannot find one champion."

CONSTANZE MOZART

1762–1842

*"Mozart was always strumming on something
—his hat, his watch fob, the table, the chair,
as if they were the keyboard."*

CONSTANZE WEBER came from a musical family and married Wolfgang Mozart at 20. The composer wrote his Great Mass in C minor for Constanze, a soprano, who sang it at the 1783 premiere.

Besides their powerful music connection, the Mozarts were kindred spirits: playful, naughty-talking spendthrifts. Illness, debt, and the itinerant musician's life took a toll on their relationship. Nevertheless, their love and her stability enabled Mozart to break the stranglehold of his money-obsessed father and realize more of his potential as composer.

After Mozart's death at 35, Constanze raised their two sons and eventually remarried. But she never forgot her quirky genius spouse.

MARIA ANNA "NANNERL" MOZART

1751–1829

OH, THOSE Mozart prodigies! Wolfgang's older sister, Nannerl, monopolized attention first with her skill on the keyboards. Then Wolfgang toddled up, composing music at age five. Father Mozart, perhaps smelling a gold mine, took the kids on the road, trotting around Europe with them for as long as three years at a stretch. Life on the road was stressful. Wolfgang caught typhoid. Nannerl fell deathly ill.

Once back home, that fateful day when Nannerl turned 14 arrived. Now deemed "a marriageable woman" by her parents and society, she was forced to give up her profession as traveling musician.

Nannerl's brother finally broke free from their micromanaging father; tragically, Nannerl could not. She let him put the kibosh on other suitors and dutifully married an elderly widower of his choice.

When Wolfgang wed, Nannerl was staggered. Their close sibling ties fell away. After his death, Nannerl read a biography of her sibling and fell apart:

"[It] completely reanimated my sisterly feelings towards my so ardently beloved brother that I was often dissolved in tears."

ANNE ROYALL AND ANN BAILEY

1769–1854 • 1742–1825

AN EARLY American journalist, Anne Royall conducted interviews and compiled them in a book, *Sketches of History, Life, and Manners in the United States*. One standout subject was a frontierswoman nicknamed Mad Ann. An English immigrant whose spouse had been killed in a battle against the Shawnee in Appalachia, Ann Bailey zestfully forded rivers and traipsed through the wilderness. She played a key role in the Indian wars, spying and making daredevil runs for ammunition to supply her settlement's garrison, Fort Lee.

Royall asked Bailey:

> *"What would the General say to you, when you safely got back to camp with your ammunition?"*

Bailey's response:

> *"Why, he'd say, 'You're a brave soldier, Ann,' and tell the men to pour me a dram of whiskey."*

To render her subjects more loquacious, Royall may have smoothed the way with spirits, too. She concluded, saying:

> *"She was fond of a dram. . . . I shall never forget Ann Bailey."*

ALESSANDRA MACINGHI STROZZI

1406-1471

A SUPERMOM of medieval Florence, Alessandra Macinghi lost her husband, Matteo Strozzi, and three of their eight children before she was 30. The family had been banished from Florence for political reasons, and loss of home and patriarch caused a major sag in the family fortunes.

Mamma's priority was to find well-heeled mates for her sons and daughters. There was one major drawback: she had to do it via the medieval postal service. Signora Strozzi's remarkable trove of letters reveals that she operated like an early Cupid.com, unfriending romantic undesirables and flattering those with the plumpest dowries and assets.

The toughest nut to crack was her son Filippo, but he finally caved in to his mother's desires and wed. Perhaps this admonition prompted him to accept a bride:

"If all men were as afraid of marriage as you are, the world would have long since died out!"

Mary "Polly" Stevenson Hewson

1739–1795

DURING BEN Franklin's years in Europe, he became fast friends with his London landlady and her daughter Mary, known as Polly. They got used to the old gent's eccentricities, such as nude sunbathing. As Polly remarked:

"He is fond of being in his Birthday Suit, and has not the least apprehension of catching cold in it."

It's just as well Polly got accustomed to males who let it all hang out. She married a doctor, William Hewson, who ran an anatomy school in their home. She and Franklin witnessed Hewson's experiments on human cadavers. Back then, corpses were more than a visual hazard. After dissecting one toxic stiff, Polly's husband died of blood poisoning, leaving her with three youngsters.

Franklin, who had a genius for friendship, thought of Polly as a daughter. Over the course of a lengthy correspondence, he persuaded the widow Hewson to move her family to Philadelphia, and the pair enjoyed their sunny relationship face-to-face for their remaining years.

Adelaide and Sally Yates

1823-1917 • 1822-1892

NORTH CAROLINA sisters Sally and Adelaide met a set of male twins at a wedding. While exchanging small talk, Adelaide said flirtatiously:

"What a pity that you who love ladies so dearly can't marry, and that two young ladies can't have such lovely husbands as you would have been."

Given that mile-wide hint, the brothers began a courteous courtship. Their names? Chang and Eng Bunker, the famous Siam-born conjoined twins. Tired of touring, the well-to-do pair had become farmers. Eventually, and not without hullabaloo from parents and others, the four-way marital coupling went ahead.

Joined by a fleshy band, the twins were able to lie side by side. Although privacy was surely lacking, the marriages thrived. An eye-popping 21 little Bunkers emerged from the two unions.

Eventually, the sisters grew testy with one another, and were installed in separate homes, which the husbands visited in turns. The twins consulted doctors worldwide, but were told they could not be separated without fatality, and abandoned the hope for surgery. After 31 years of marriage to the sisters, the twins died on the same day. Sally and Adelaide became widows—but finally got some longed-for privacy!

ISABELLA D'ESTE

1474–1539

BRAINY, RESTLESS Isabella d'Este of Mantua, Italy, wrote more than 12,000 letters, by hand. Some hint at the brutality of the times, such as this one to a master craftsman:

"We are glad to hear that you are doing your utmost to finish our studiolo, *so as not be sent to prison."*

The *studiolo* and her *grotta*, famous rooms within the d'Este ducal palace, were the talk of Italy. When not browbeating underlings, Isabella was a devoted patron of the Renaissance. She collected antiquities and commissioned a large amount of fine art. She also started Italian fashion trends, including a fad for dresses with nipple-revealing décolletage.

CLARA WIECK SCHUMANN

1819–1896

A PIANO prodigy, Clara Wieck played professionally at five, touring Europe as the first pianist to perform from memory. She also wrote music, and said of this pursuit:

"Composing gives me great pleasure . . . there is nothing that surpasses the joy of creation."

She was one of many musical geniuses Germany produced at the time; another was Robert Schumann, whom Clara wed at 21. Eventually, with eight childish mouths to feed, she remained the breadwinner as a concert pianist, pushing her husband's composing talent ahead of hers.

After 15 years of marriage, Robert was confined to a psychiatric hospital, and died when Clara was 35. She continued her concert career for decades but had lost her zest for writing music:

"I once believed that I possessed creative talent, but I have given up this idea; a woman must not desire to compose."

MICHITSUNA NO HAHA

CA. 935-995

A JAPANESE noblewoman known only as Michitsuna no Haha, or "Michitsuna's mother," authored an early novel called *The Mayfly Diary* or *The Gossamer Years*. Presented as a personal diary of the lush Heian period, it captures 21 years of a marriage more bitter than sweet, filled with the ache caused by infidelities and female rivals. Michitsuna no Haha's words are timeless, managing to erase the centuries since she penned them:

"I felt as though I could not let things stand as they were. Early the next morning I sent, attached to a withered chrysanthemum, a poem written with more care than usual.

'Do you know how slow the dawn can be when you have to wait alone?'"

JULIA WARD HOWE

1819–1910

AFTER MEETING President Lincoln, Julia Ward Howe felt so moved that she obliged when a friend challenged her to write an inspiring poem overnight. She scribbled the words in the dark, not wanting to wake her small baby. The stirring verses of the "Battle Hymn of the Republic" were the result. Howe sent the piece to her editor at the *Atlantic Monthly*, who paid her $5. Published in 1862, it impressed the readership and became the Union's heartfelt anthem.

A multifaceted writer and a genial activist, Howe triumphed professionally but considered her marriage a failure. From the get-go, her husband disputed her choice to have a career outside of wife and mother. On their 22nd anniversary, she wrote in her journal:

"I have never known my husband to approve any act of mine which I myself valued. Books—poems—essays—everything has been contemptible or contraband in his eyes, because it was not his way of doing things."

ABIGAIL ADAMS

1744–1818

A DELIGHTFUL motormouth, First Lady Abigail Adams spent years writing to her husband, John Adams, the second US president, who was often sent abroad as America's representative. Although Abigail was sometimes housebound with five offspring, she got unusual pleasure out of their decades-long correspondence, as did he. Her carefully copied letters, which survive, range from witty asides to feisty rebuttals on everything from wartime profiteering to her much-quoted riffs on female equality. As for the value of the open communication she enjoyed with John, she was clear:

"My pen is always freer than my tongue,
for I have written many things to you that
I suppose I never would have talked."

ALESSANDRA BOCCHINERI

CA. 1610–1650

ALTHOUGH A dazzler, Alessandra had a troubled life and was on her third husband when she struck it lucky. When her sister married Vincenzo Gamba Galilei, Alessandra began a decade-long pen-pal relationship with Galileo Galilei, Vincenzo's father, who remained under house arrest for his Church-quaking theories. One of her notes reveals how deep the friendship became:

*"I often wonder how I'll be able,
before I die, to find a way to be with you
and spend a day in conversation, without
scandalizing . . . those people who have
made fun of us for this wish."*

Although their relationship remained long-distance, she lit up Galileo's final days; he wrote his last letter on earth to her.

ZINA D. H. YOUNG

1821–1901

ZINA YOUNG, a member of one of the families that fled west with Mormon founder Joseph Smith, received two marriage proposals in 1841. One was from Henry Jacobs, whom she promptly wed. The second came from the already-married Smith. Won over by the latter's pro-polygamy platform, Zina submitted to his request as well, though by then she was already pregnant by early-bird Jacobs.

Three years later, Smith bit the dust and Jacobs left on a church mission. Zina sealed a third nuptial deal, this time with Brigham Young, Smith's successor, who claimed his forebear's wives as his property.

As a church leader, Zina regularly lectured the wives, including Brigham's lineup. She was apparently the only one of the women to undertake polyandry (having multiple male mates). Zina may have savored the variety or found it burdensome. Mormon-style intimacy wasn't supposed to be fun, as Zina emphasized:

"[The wife] must regard her husband with indifference . . . for love we regard as a false sentiment; a feeling which should have no existence in polygamy."

CHAPTER SIX

RISK TAKERS AND
ROAMERS

SOPHIE DE CONDORCET

1764–1822

ALTHOUGH BURDENED at birth with the surname "de Grouchy," Sophie was *magnifique*. She became Madame de Condorcet through marriage, but her aristocratic mate lost his life during the Reign of Terror before the French Revolution.

Despite widowhood, loss of fortune, and political turmoil, Sophie carried on, translating works of Thomas Paine and other writers into French and encouraging women's rights. Sophie even had the guts to confront Napoleon when he groused about women who dabbled in politics:

"You're right, General. But in a country where their heads are cut off, it is natural they should wish to know the reason why."

ELEANOR "NELL" GWYN
1650-1687

BORN ON London's seedy side, Nell hawked oranges in the-aters as a teen. She soon became famous for snappy comebacks, and her earthy wit led to comic roles onstage.

After Gwyn became a favorite mistress of King Charles II, Londoners once mistook her coach for that of a rival, the very Catholic Duchess of Portsmouth. As the crowd shouted rude words, Nell poked her head from the coach to say:

"Good people, be civil—
I am the Protestant *whore!"*

SARAH KEMBLE KNIGHT

1666–1727

AN AGILE and bold businesswoman, the widowed Sarah Kemble Knight undertook a solo five-month horseback journey through the wilderness of 17th-century New England in order to settle some legal affairs. While facing down hazards galore, from raging rivers to drunken louts at inns, she recorded it all in a journal.

Some of Knight's insights sound uncannily modern. She noted the ease with which the native peoples she encountered obtained a divorce:

> *"In either side, saying 'stand away' to one another is a sufficient Divorce. And indeed those uncomely 'Stand aways' are too much in Vogue among the English in this (Indulgent Colony) as their Records plentifully prove."*

Knight's reporting was accurate. During an era when divorce was all but impossible, newspapers were filled with accounts of white men and women who fled their families.

PHRYNE OF THESPIAE

CA. 371–316 BC

BORN DIRT poor in the ancient Greek city of Thespiae, Phryne took her assets to Athens. Her splendid figure made her a favorite of the sculptor Praxiteles, and she is said to have been the model for his nude statue *Aphrodite of Knidos*.

Phryne also moonlighted as a courtesan and was known for her wit. After a friend brought her a stingy amount of good wine, boasting it had aged for a decade, she drawled:

*"It's small indeed, considering how
many years old it is!"*

CATHERINE SEDLEY

1657–1717

A SERIAL sexual adventurer during the anything-goes era of the English king Charles II, Catherine Sedley could count among her assets wit, audacity, and an inheritance from her father. As mistress of the Duke of York, who became King James II, she received a title upgrade, becoming Duchess of Dorchester.

At 38, however, Catherine quit her post as mistress. To general astonishment, she wed a Scottish army vet and raised two sons. Frank about her past, Sedley frequently reminded her boys of their place as they grew, and gave them this sound advice:

"If any body should call you sons of a whore, you must bear it, for you are so. But if they call you bastards, fight till you die; for you are an honest man's sons."

BIRGITTA OF SWEDEN

1303–1373

A MOTHER of eight, a mystic who led pilgrimages, and the founder of a religious order that at one time had 80 convents throughout Europe, Birgitta (or Bridget) of Sweden is one of Europe's patron saints. She documented her 700-plus visions, and her published *Revelations* are still widely read. Her blonde beauty often served as a model for the Virgin Mary in medieval art.

Never holier than thou, Birgitta projected down-to-earth warmth. She loved to laugh, and apparently she enjoyed Mediterranean *vino* as well:

"Wine is wholesome, gives health to the sick, joy to the sorrowful, courage and bravery to those who are well."

MARIA SIBYLLA MERIAN
1647–1717

GERMAN NATURALIST and illustrator Maria Merian closely studied insect metamorphosis, collecting live specimens and observing species in nature. She was considered somewhat batty, as illustrators and scientists in her day normally worked from dead, dried specimens. Like the caterpillars she admired, Merian transformed herself—shedding her husband and marital life.

After she wrote and illustrated *The Wonderful Transformation and Singular Plant-Food of Caterpillars*, Merian longed to see splashier insects. She made a voyage to Suriname, South America, at the time a colony of the Netherlands.

Despite the humid, malarial conditions, Maria went bonkers for the bugs. She was equally stunned by the brutal lives of the Suriname slaves. She made the following observation in *Metamorphosis Insectorum Surinamensium*, the book that made her reputation:

"Indians, who are not well treated in their servitude by the Dutch, use [the peacock flower's seeds] to abort their children so that they will not become slaves like them."

MARGARET CATCHPOLE

1762–1819

A SWEET-TALKING guy and a moment of weakness led an amateur horse thief named Catchpole to a one-way convicts' cruise to Australia, dumping ground for England's criminals. (In the early 1800s, even a minor shoplifting charge could put you on a ship to Down Under.)

Margaret Catchpole warmed to the terrain, however, marveled at the Aussie wildlife, and became a midwife and gardener. She wrote lively, detailed letters to the folks back home, in which she provided one of the few eyewitness reports of the great Hawkesbury River flood of 1806. As the waters rose, she scrambled onto a housetop, describing the scene in one of her letters:

"We'd not been there long before the chimney . . . and middle wall went. . . . I expected to be crushed to death. . . . A boat [saved] us from a watery grave."

NANCY KELSEY

1823–1896

"Where my husband goes, I can go. I can better endure the hardships of the journey than the anxiety of an absent husband."

The pioneering Kelsey family wandered from Missouri to California to Oregon, most of the time without a compass or guide. Nancy, the family matriarch and one tough cookie, gave birth 10 times while following her wanderlust-driven husband.

Among her many adventures was participation in the Bear Flag Revolt. She hand-painted the bear on the funky flag raised for California's first "declaration of independence" from Mexico. For 24 raucous days, Nancy Kelsey helped stake a claim to the Bear Flag Republic, until the Feds spoiled the fun by showing up and planting the US standard instead.

ANNIE SMITH PECK

1850–1935

ARCHAEOLOGIST AND college professor Annie Smith Peck discovered the joys of high-altitude climbing in her 30s. She summited some of the smaller Alps and then tackled a couple of Greek peaks, followed by California's Mount Shasta in 1888. After Peck had ascended the Matterhorn—provoking gasps for wearing trousers to climb—she decided to break some new ground:

> *"My next thought was to do a little genuine exploration to conquer a virgin peak, to attain some height where no man had previously stood."*

In 1904, she found a Peruvian mountain that provided the challenge she sought. It took six treacherous attempts before Peck, at age 60, scaled 22,205-foot Mount Huascarán. In 1914, she mischievously planted a "Women's Vote" banner on a neighboring peak.

HANNAH CALLOWHILL PENN

1671–1726

BEING HANNAH Callowhill Penn took boundless energy: besides bearing six children, she endured a number of ghastly three-month voyages to and from the New World. A Quaker with a good head for spreadsheets, she managed the English colony of Pennsylvania while her loving husband, William Penn, was rendered unable, first by debtors' prison, then by a stroke, and finally by death.

Hannah walked a tightrope, fighting for financial stability of the colony while protecting the precious civil rights that her husband had fought for. When she was away in England, she ordered an advisor left behind:

"Pray do nothing of consequence without [my] order . . . for the people [of Pennsylvania colony] are safe and therefore I would have them think themselves so . . . their comfort is so near interwoven with mine."

Hannah Callowhill Penn's proprietorship was honored in 2014 with official recognition as the state's first female governor.

HESTER STANHOPE

1776–1839

HESTER STANHOPE segued from a post as hostess for her uncle, the British prime minister, to high-end vagabond. Around 1810, she began her own odyssey by getting shipwrecked near Greece. After losing her wardrobe and other possessions, Lady Stanhope breezily adopted the flowing robes worn by the Turks, even going unveiled as she wandered through the desert to Damascus, Syria.

Stanhope had found paradise—and her self-described role in life as Queen of the Desert. In her journals, she burbled:

> *"I'm the oracle of the place, the darling of all the troops, who seem to think I am a deity because I can ride, and because I bear arms."*

Lady Stanhope survived plague and eventual poverty, during which she was fed by kind Arabs who viewed her as their very own madwoman oracle.

LILLIE LANGTRY

1853–1929

A LIGHTWEIGHT actress, Lillie clicked with American and British theatergoers. Although married twice, she became better known as a serial mistress for a lineup of (mostly) distinguished gents.

Among them was "Bertie," Prince of Wales and prime philanderer of the royal family, who would later hand off his crown to wed Wallis Simpson. He ranked high on Lillie's paramour list. He built a private retreat for their affair, and once complained to her, "I've spent enough on you to build a battleship."

Lillie pertly replied:

"And you've spent enough in me to float one!"

When a friend asked whether the prince was a romantic lover, Lillie smiled:

"Not at all—just a straightaway pounder!"

LAIS OF GREECE

DIED 340 BC

LAIS WAS a Greek *hetaira*, or sexual companion. Often quoted by contemporaries for her clever mind, Lais was rumored to have time-share arrangements with the philosophers she favored, Aristippus and Diogenes the Cynic. She charged the former top drachma, but slept with Diogenes for free, since he owned nothing.

Regarding her relationships with intellectuals, she said, perhaps with a wink:

"I don't understand what is meant by the 'austerity' of philosophers . . . they are just as much in my power as the rest of the citizens."

ELIZABETH CLEGHORN GASKELL

1810–1865

"A man is so in the way in the house."

That sprightly comment came from *Cranford*, an 1853 novel by Elizabeth Gaskell. Early in her career, as a fan of Charles Dickens, Elizabeth asked the world-famous author's advice about helping a girl she had visited in prison. Because of their mutual involvement in social justice and popular literature, Dickens gave Gaskell a golden opportunity: he published her work in serial form in his weekly journal.

That attention brought further perks. Mrs. Gaskell entered Dickens's lineup of ghost-story writers. In addition, the head of the Brontë family, the rock-star writers of the era, tapped Elizabeth to write a biography of Charlotte Brontë.

MARGARET FULLER

1810–1850

"Woman is the flower, man the bee. She sighs out melodious fragrance, and invites the winged laborer. He drains her cup, and carries off the honey. She dies on the stalk; he returns to the hive, well fed, and praised as an active member of the community."

Margaret Fuller may have gotten the science wrong, but her sentiments were right. Author of the feminist tract *Woman in the Nineteenth Century*, she wrote mercilessly honest prose that stung as well as sang.

Fuller was a successful journalist. As America's first female foreign correspondent, writing for the *New York Tribune*, she covered the revolutionary actions in Italy in the late 1840s that led to the Risorgimento, as the reunification of Italy was called. In 1850 Fuller sailed home, returning with the new loves of her life, an Italian revolutionary and their infant son, and eager to write about the exciting women's movement. Nearing New York, their ship hit a sandbar off Fire Island and sank. All three of them drowned.

RAYMONDE DE LAROCHE

CA. 1882–1919

A FRENCH plumber's daughter, Raymonde de Laroche went mad for aeronautics. A hot-air balloonist, she took up fixed-wing flying one year after the Wright brothers' historic flight. As an encore, she became the world's first woman to get a pilot's license.

Like other daredevils in this new field, de Laroche crashed multiple times, sustaining serious injuries. After being grounded during World War I, Raymonde became airborne again, setting altitude (15,700 feet) and distance (201 miles) records. By then she longed to be a test pilot, and died in an experimental aircraft, doing what she loved. Risks be damned, Raymonde often asserted, claiming:

"Flying is the best possible
thing for women."

CHRISTIAN DAVIES

1667–1739

LATE IN life, Christian Davies recounted that even as a girl, she had been drawn to the unfeminine:

"[I preferred] Manly Employments, such as handling a rake, flail, pitchfork, [and] riding horses bareback."

She still enjoyed these pursuits as an adult, and when her husband got drafted into the British infantry, she parked her kids with family and went to track down her man. Davies donned male breeches and military jacket:

"[I took] care to quilt the Waistcoat, to preserve my Breasts from hurt which were not large enough to betray my Sex."

Ten years and countless misadventures later, Davies found her husband, expiring on a Flanders battlefield. By now she'd fought in two countries, used various aliases, been a POW, and relished the unhygienic macho life.

Eventually, she ran out of conflicts. As a civilian, Christian opened a tavern and pie shop in Dublin, remarried, and often traveled, relishing her status as a war heroine.

CHRISTINA OF DENMARK

1521–1590

BEFORE SELFIES—indeed, before photography existed at all—royal males who wanted a glimpse of a prospective mate before an arranged marriage had another option: send a portrait painter, such as Hans Holbein, to the woman in question.

In 1538, English king Henry VIII was wife hunting, again. When Holbein returned with an image of Denmark's dimpled young duchess (who had been widowed at 13!), Henry was smitten. Negotiations began. The English ambassador laid it on thick, assuring her Henry was "a Gentleman, his nature benign and pleasant."

Well aware of the king's vicious track record, Christina was said to have responded:

"If I had two heads, I'd be happy to offer
King Henry one of them!"

LOUISE CLAPPE

1819–1906

SETTLING THE West could be grievously hard, but some women, such as Louise Clappe, relished it. Her doctor husband practiced medicine in a rough-and-tumble gold-mining camp. Her house was a tent. Despite the discomforts, she wrote to her sister:

"I like this wild and barbarous life."

Louise's impressions of that life would later be published as *The Dame Shirley Letters*. They included this recommendation:

"Everybody ought to go to the mines,
just to see how little it takes to make people
comfortable in the world."

NELLIE BLY

1864–1922

INTRIGUED BY the flair of a young letter-to-the-editor writer named Elizabeth Cochrane, a Pittsburgh editor offered her a reporting gig and a pen name, Nellie Bly. She made a name as a crack investigative journalist, and after taking a job in New York even did undercover work, infiltrating an insane asylum by posing as a mental patient. But Bly got even more attention from her round-the-world stunt.

The gimmick was to outdo the fictional protagonist of Jules Verne's best-selling *Around the World in 80 Days*. Traveling 25,000 miles by ship, train, bus, rickshaw, horseback, and burro, Nellie returned home to cheering crowds in 72 days, six hours, and 11 minutes.

Reporters sought quotes from her about how she succeeded in her "race against time." Perhaps saving her best lines for her own work, Bly said, simply:

"Never having failed, I could not
picture what failure meant."

ISABELLA BIRD

1831–1904

AT 21, Isabella Bird contracted an incurable disease: the travel bug. She had felt suffocated by English conventional life and had frequently been physically ill. On one of her long sea journeys, as her ship encountered storms off New Zealand, the neophyte vagabond wrote to her sister, Henrietta:

> *"The old Sea God has stolen my heart*
> *and penetrated my soul . . . [it is] like*
> *living in a new world, so pure, so fresh, so vital,*
> *so careless, so unfettered. . . . I cannot tell*
> *you how much I like my life!"*

Globetrotting for the next half century, Isabella wrote worthy books about her adventures; at 61 she became the first woman invited to join the Royal Geographical Society.

DAISY BATES

1859–1951

WITHOUT TRYING to convert or teach, Irish journalist Daisy Bates lived among Aborigines in the Australian Outback for 40 years, gaining acceptance by learning their languages.

Bates had her own secrets: she had married three men without bothering to divorce any of them. Her first spouse had been the Second Boer War commander, war criminal, and folk hero Breaker Morant.

Although kitted out in prissy Edwardian duds, Daisy was as tough as kangaroo leather. Roaming the harsh land, she wrote lengthy reports for the *London Times* and completed a small masterpiece called *Passing of the Aborigines*.

Without batting an eyelash or mussing her best bib and tucker, Bates observed circumcision ceremonies, cannibalism, and other rituals of the tribes she moved with, many of them outcasts from their traditional lands. Opposed to interracial absorption, she mourned their future disappearance:

"There is no hope for tomorrow, but I can
help each one of them for today."

JANE AUSTEN

1775–1817

IF JANE showed up today, she'd be flabbergasted at the kudos, the copycats, and the astonishing cash thrown at all things Austen.

Jane Austen's fortunes had their ups and downs, as they were often dependent upon the generosity of relatives. Her father and brother promoted her writing; four of her novels were published in her lifetime (although anonymously) and brought in modest royalties.

Despite the central role of marriage in her novels, the author declined to marry. That she was as lively and witty as her novels can be gleaned from this quip in a Christmas letter to her sister Cassandra:

"I do not want people to be very agreeable, as it saves me the trouble of liking them a great deal."

MARY RAMSEY "GRANNY" WOOD

1787/1810–1908

A HIGH-VITALITY pioneer born in Tennessee, Mary Ramsey Wood outlived two husbands while moving ever westward. Eventually, with the families of two of her children, she made it to Oregon. Legend has it that she rode a mare all the way. As a youth, it is said, she danced with Andrew Jackson and saw Thomas Jefferson in the flesh. As a centenarian (or nearly one—her birthdate is reported variously as early as 1787 and as late as 1810), while preparing for the hereafter, Granny Wood instructed her family:

> *"Whatever you do, don't convey my
> remains in a hearse! Load my coffin in
> a hack. I've lived as a Democrat and
> I'll go out in a Democratic wagon."*

CHAPTER SEVEN

DILEMMAS, CLOSE CALLS, AND DIRE STRAITS

ANNIE EDSON TAYLOR

1838–1921

DESPERATE FOR money, Civil War widow Annie Edson Taylor risked a harrowing publicity stunt, becoming the first person to go over Niagara Falls in a barrel—and survive. The trip in a reinforced, weighted barrel from upriver to below the cascade took less than 20 minutes; it just seemed like an eternity. After attending to minor injuries and catching her breath, Taylor, a 63-year-old dance teacher, said:

> *"Nobody ought ever to
> do that again."*

POLICARPA SALAVARRIETA

CA. 1795–1817

A SOUTH American freedom fighter, Policarpa Salavarrieta took big risks in New Granada (today's Colombia) during the battle for independence from Spain. La Pola, as she was known, spied, hustled funds, and organized sister collaborators, who recruited soldiers and materials for the resistance movement.

In 1817, things went sour; the young woman was captured by Spanish forces and brusquely sent to the firing squad. Unbroken, Policarpa yelled to the crowd:

"How different our fate would be today
if you truly knew the price of liberty!"

Two years later, her homeland won its freedom from Spain. This warrior-martyr is fondly remembered today, pictured on Colombian banknotes and honored on Bogotá's annual Day of Colombian Women.

SARAH AND DORCAS GOOD

1653–1692 • BORN CA. 1687

DURING THE witch hunts of Salem, Massachusetts, as an indigent local named Sarah Good was about to be hanged, a minister urged her to make a last-minute confession. Sarah, defiant to the end, cried:

> *"I am no more a witch than you are*
> *a wizard! If you take my life away,*
> *God will give you blood to drink."*

Salem's accusers had gone beyond hysteria. Not only did they hang Sarah, they imprisoned her daughter, Dorcas (or Dorothy, in some accounts), who had supposedly "confessed" to being Satan's helper. Kept in vile conditions for nine months, Dorcas was finally released. She was five years old.

In 1711, the people of Massachusetts, abashed at the wrongs done to Good and others, tried to make amends. They awarded funds to the survivors. Dorcas, now 24 or 25, and her father got 30 pounds. Tardy as it was, the gesture may have helped heal the scars sustained by Salem's youngest purported witch.

MARTHA WASHINGTON

1731–1802

WIFE OF the first US president, Martha Washington did not set a benchmark for other First Ladies to follow. A wealthy, slave-owning Virginian, Martha loved George but was opposed to his presidency and refused to attend his inauguration.

During the Revolutionary War years, she had made morale-raising trips to his army's winter encampment. But she was more reluctant about performing White House wifely duties now considered vital, such as fake smiles and purely positive remarks. As Lady Washington once grumped to a friend:

"I live a very dull life here . . . indeed I think I am more like a state prisoner than anything else."

ADA KING, COUNTESS OF LOVELACE

1815–1852

ADA KING, now dubbed the first computer programmer by adoring cyber-geeks, got an early start in math and science. At 17, she met Charles Babbage and quickly grasped the ideas behind his wonky number-crunching device, the Analytical Engine. She wrote a program as well as commentaries explaining his concept, and Babbage dubbed her "the enchantress of numbers."

The brainy countess, a daughter of Lord Byron, grasped the potential of such a tool to compute as well as calculate:

"The Analytical Engine weaves algebraic
patterns just as the Jacquard-loom
weaves flowers and leaves."

Ada, who loved gambling as well as equations, field tested her mathematical theories by creating a system for winning bets. It failed, and she spun the wheel of misfortune instead. The enchantress of numbers died of uterine cancer at 37, deeply in debt.

ANNA BELKNAP

1833–1880

IN 1848, Anna Belknap and other hardy souls were home-steading in Oregon's fertile Willamette Valley when the news hit—gold had been discovered in California! The men went wild, the stories growing with each telling. Within weeks, all able-bodied males had headed south—many never to return.

In her journal, Anna, a clear-eyed realist, assessed the damage:

> *"If it had not been for our Indian neighbors, not many of us could have survived. Gold broke up more homes in that day and age than alcohol ever did."*

MARGARET "MOLLY" BROWN

1867–1932

A NUMBER of survivors of the 1912 *Titanic* disaster owed their lives to Margaret Brown's quick-witted leadership during and after the iceberg collision. She helped load women and children into the precious few lifeboats, grabbed an oar, and incited the other women into rowing also. Her lawyer was astonished to receive a telegram that said in part:

"Neptune was exceedingly kind to me and I am now high and dry."

Once the survivors boarded the rescue ship *Carpathia*, Mrs. Brown, who was dubbed "unsinkable Molly" after her death, organized a Survivors' Committee, raising nearly $10,000 for those left destitute. Irate at learning that she (being female) could not testify at the *Titanic* hearings, Brown sent her own version of events to US newspapers.

Margaret, who began life as a ditch digger's daughter, had sought adventure in Colorado as a young woman, long before that fateful cruise. She hit pay dirt, marrying a miner who discovered a million-dollar mother lode. Brown was a decidedly eccentric but compassionate woman with survival smarts. If only the *Titanic*'s captain had behaved half as well.

MARIE-JEANNE "MANON" ROLAND

1754–1793

IN THE turmoil of late 18th-century France, keeping track of revolutionaries and counter-revolutionaries was tricky. As Girondin party leaders, Madame Roland and her bureaucrat spouse, Jean-Marie, had at first enjoyed civil relations with the rival Jacobins. But animosity arose, and when mob rule took over, she was forced into the conga line to the guillotine. When she stepped up to the awful blade, Madame Roland cried:

"Oh, liberty! What crimes are
committed in your name!"

CLARA MAASS

1876–1901

"Don't worry, Mother, if you hear I have yellow fever. Most of the cases are mild, and [afterward] I should be immune and not be afraid of the disease anymore."

A century ago, yellow fever usually meant a painful death. Walter Reed, the first doctor to prove that mosquito bites transmitted the illness, asked for volunteers for an immunity experiment. Clara Maass stepped up. As a nurse, she'd treated hundreds of soldiers ill with yellow fever during the Spanish-American war.

The experiment began. Maass got a mild case, but Reed and the other medicos opted to inflict a second mosquito bite, to see whether she had immunity. She did not, and the disease killed her. Clara's death spurred the drive for cures and prevention. Her sacrifice was small comfort to her mother, who had been depending on half of her daughter's $10 monthly paycheck.

ANN BATES

CA. 1748–1790

WHO SAYS women can't emulate James Bond? When the American Revolutionary War broke out, British loyalist Bates quit her teaching job and took on the guise of "peddler Ann." Infiltrating George Washington's military camps, she sold combs and medicinal rhubarb while counting cannons and assessing Yankee manpower. Her spying talent won her lavish praise.

When the Redcoats got hammered, however, and Bates returned to England, she began her own battle to get the pension promised to her. It took ages, but her indignant dunning eventually got results. Perhaps the king's men didn't care for the light she cast them in with this statement:

"Haid I Doon half as much for the Scruff of Mankind, I mean the Rabls [American rebels], I Should not be thus Left to Parish."

MARY ANNING

1799–1847

IN MARY Anning's day, paleontology was a budding science. Her family lived near a cliffside formation laid down in the late Triassic and early Jurassic periods, possibly the richest fossil site in Britain. The Anning family collected and sold fossils as curios.

After sharp-eyed Mary and her brother found an ichthyosaur skeleton in 1810, their work drew more attention. Mentored by her keenest customers, Mary became very knowledgeable about prehistoric species. The fieldwork she did was dangerous; the cliffs were subject to deadly landslides, and in 1833, she was nearly killed by one that buried her terrier.

By then Mary had more advanced knowledge than many of her educated clients; she even submitted corrections to scientific articles. Although Anning's pioneering work is well appreciated today, being poor and female in 19th-century England meant she never gained acceptance and very often was denied credit for her discoveries. Before dying of cancer at 47, she wrote a heartrending farewell:

"The world has used me so unkindly, I fear it has made me suspicious of everyone."

ERISTI-AYA

ACTIVE CA. 1695 BC

MESOPOTAMIAN ROYALS Queen Shibtu and King Zimri-Lin had at least seven daughters. They decided their youngest, Eristi-Aya, should become a priestess at a temple miles from their palace at Mari. It was a teen dream of a job: light religious duties, fancy wardrobe, even a shopping allowance.

Eristi-Aya couldn't phone or text, but, boy, did she hound her parents. Her clay tablet letters (later translated by amused archaeologists) were unrelenting. A typical complaint:

"I am always crying out, always! When I wrote you last year, you sent me two slaves but one of them died. Now they've brought two more slaves, and one of them had to go and die! . . . Why am I not getting my allowances of oil and honey?"

ELIZABETH DRINKER

1735–1807

A PHILADELPHIA Quaker and diarist, Elizabeth Drinker filled 36 volumes with 50 years of commentary. Her historically priceless record of colonial life reveals the touching bravery of colonials in the face of their vast ignorance about hygiene and contagious disease, and the harebrained remedies they clung to. Of yellow fever she wrote:

"A Fever prevails in the City . . . of ye malignant kind; numbers have died of it. Some say it was occasioned by damaged Coffee and Fish. They have burnt Tar in ye Streets, and taken many other precautions."

Daily bathing was also a nonstarter for early Americans, who lacked decent soap, running water, and tubs. Drinker's husband, perhaps longing for a squeaky-clean mate, built a rustic shower box and invited her to use it. Elizabeth queasily submitted, later reporting:

"I bore it better than I expected, not having been wett all over att once, for 28 years past."

ARGULA VON GRUMBACH

1492–CA. 1563

A GERMAN intellectual and a Lutheran during Martin Luther's lifetime, Argula von Grumbach found herself in trouble for defending a Protestant teacher at the university in Bavaria. After sending letters to the school, city council, and Luther himself, she got just one response: a scurrilous, anonymous poem that mocked her opinions, hinting that she had the hots for the educator in question. Argula responded with wit and unflinching courage:

> *"I'm distressed that our princes*
> *take the Word of God no more seriously*
> *than a cow does a game of chess."*

In spite of that setback, von Grumbach was undeterred. Her intelligently written arguments continued to be printed and distributed widely by reformers—and to cause no end of ruckus.

ELIZABETH VAN LEW

1818–1900

A SOUTHERN belle in a plush Virginia mansion, Elizabeth Van Lew lived the good life. It was a double life, however, as she was against slavery and for the Union. Her only confidante was her diary. When fighting between the North and South began, this philanthropic Virginian took big risks. Elizabeth gave POWs food and medicine, and ran a spy network of women, black and white. Her daring group circulated messages through multiple hiding places. Her work and theirs won General Grant's lavish praise after the war.

But Richmonders and other Southerners never forgave Van Lew for her treachery. As she wrote in her diary (the existence of which was revealed on her deathbed):

"I'm held in contempt & scorn by the narrow minded men and women of my city. . . . living utterly alone in the city of my birth, as if I spoke a different language."

MARGARET BAYNHAM

ACTIVE 1545

MARKETING MAVEN Margaret Baynham juggled enterprises on both sides of the English Channel. From England, she annually exported 20,000 pounds of wool. In Calais, Baynham ran a boardinghouse and exported French wine and herring. Writing to business partners, twice-widowed Margaret shares everyday tragedies and her stoic acceptance:

"I heartily thank you for the good beer you sent . . . albeit a great part . . . hath been drunk amid lamentation and mourning. Palm Sunday we perceived that John Crant was sick of the plague, whereupon I and all my household were glad to void my house . . . one of my sister's daughters, waxed suddenly sick of the same disease. . . . Thus doth God chastise and scourge me . . . to keep me in awe and under correction still."

ARTEMISIA GENTILESCHI

1593–1652

BLESSED WITH talent, cursed with a clueless father, Italian painter Artemisia Gentileschi gained notoriety after her instructor sexually assaulted her. The thuggish artist who committed the crime, Agostino Tassi, turned out to have a rap sheet that included murder.

Gentileschi's father took Tassi to court, and the whole nasty affair went public. After the 19-year-old endured an invasive examination of her private parts by two midwives, she faced a further ordeal. In that brutal age, witnesses were routinely tortured to elicit the truth. A potentially crippling device called the sybille was attached to Artemisia's fingers, cutting off her circulation.

The trial lasted five months, shredding Artemisia's reputation but not her spirit. She left Rome for Florence, joined the painters' guild, and took up her brushes again. Painting became her therapy. Artemisia's unbowed attitude and pride in her work carried her through life, despite salacious gossip and haggling patrons. As she wrote to one such patron:

"You will find the spirit of Caesar
in the soul of this woman."

KATHERINE MANSFIELD

1888–1923

*"Don't lower your mask until you have another
mask prepared beneath—as terrible as
you like—but a mask."*

Talent, tragedy, and mystery thread through the life of New
Zealand writer Katherine Mansfield, known for her short-story
output, bohemian friendships, and complex love affairs.

While in her 20s, Katherine contracted tuberculosis.
Seeking a cure, she allowed a doctor to bombard her spleen with
X-rays. Later, to heal spiritually if not physically, she studied
with disciples of the Armenian guru George Gurdjieff.

When Mansfield died at 35, her spouse, John Middleton
Murry, edited her journals with a heavy hand before publishing
them and her letters. Despite his meddling, Katherine's searing
words often unmasked the truth.

Louise Elisabeth Vigée Le Brun

1755–1842

THE PROLIFIC and terrific Louise Le Brun painted 662 portraits and other works. By her 30s, she had earned over a million francs, most of which her husband frittered away. Her most memorable works were the 25 portraits she made of Marie-Antoinette while painter-in-ordinary to the queen.

The two became fast friends. Louise knew the warm, affectionate woman behind the artificial queenly mask. She made it her business to defend Marie-Antoinette and overturn her reputation as cold and uncaring. To that end, she painted the famous portrait of the queen with her children, and she reported of her friend:

> *"Marie-Antoinette never missed an opportunity of saying something pleasant to those who had the honor of being presented to her."*

Le Brun's help wasn't adequate; nothing was. The turbulent times needed a scapegoat, and the Austrian-born queen of France was it.

Marie Tussaud

1761–1850

Marie Tussaud had an artist's eye and a magician's fingers. Mentored by a master sculptor, young Marie made wax portraits of such French celebrities as Voltaire. When the bloody Reign of Terror began, however, Tussaud went to prison. Later released, she landed the grisly job of making death masks from freshly severed noggins—including that of Marie-Antoinette.

When she was able, Madame Tussaud fled France for England, where she created the first of several waxwork museums. In her memoirs, she revealed the Gallic horrors she had narrowly escaped:

"The royal prisoners were compelled
to have their hair closely cut every week,
in order that their heads might be . . .
fit for the guillotines."

NINON DE LENCLOS

1616–1706

A TOP-TIER French courtesan, Ninon de Lenclos was mistress to royals, generals, and a randy abbot or two. Her career went swimmingly for years, discreetly interrupted a few times for childbirth. In 1659, however, Anne of Austria, regent for Louis XIV during his minority, took issue with Lenclos's religious skepticism and sent her into convent lockup. There she wrote her memoirs, concealing her journal in her underwear until she found a publisher. Among its memorable lines:

"We should take care to lay in a stock of provisions, but not of pleasures; these should be gathered day by day."

Upon release, Ninon gleefully returned to her hedonistic life. One often-told story relates that she became intimate, unbeknownst to her or him, with her own son, who had been raised by his father's family. Upon discovering their connection, he committed suicide. If true, the tragedy would have left her heartbroken. In any event, Ninon was condemned to a cruel fate for a beauty: she lived to be 90, leaving behind this rueful one-liner:

"Old age is woman's hell."

VIRGINIA REED

1833–1921

VIRGINIA REED was a 13-year-old member of the Donner Party, whose westward-bound journey went terribly wrong. Trapped for months in snowy mountains due to delays, loss of wagons, and weather, the starving survivors were reduced to gnawing hides and, in some cases, to eating the flesh of their dead fellows.

Plucky Virginia wrote a long, shattering letter to her cousin after their ordeal, explaining some of the horrors faced:

"We had to kill little cash the dog & eat him, we ate his entrails & feet & hide & evry thing about him o my dear Cousin you don't know what trubel is yet . . . thay was 11 days without any thing to eat but the Dead."

TAMSEN DONNER

1801–1847

THE DONNER Party of 87 would be snowbound in California's Sierra Nevada for five months. Did George Donner's wife, Tamsen, have a premonition of the terror that lay ahead? At the Platte River in June, she wrote a letter to a friend that included this excerpt:

"Our preparations for the journey . . .
might have been bettered. We laid in 150 lbs. of
flour and 75 lbs. of meat for each individual,
and I fear bread will be scarce."

After the party took a seldom-tried alternative route, disaster hit. Half the group perished. Tamsen refused to leave her dying husband despite the pleas of several sets of rescuers. Later, the Donner Party's last survivor confessed to having cannibalized her remains.

LOUISA JOHNSON ADAMS

1775–1852

IN THE winter of 1815, Louisa Adams, the wife of an American diplomat, and her young son were obliged to set out with a handful of servants from Saint Petersburg, Russia, to Paris. In a horse-drawn sleigh, they spent 40 grueling days traveling through 1,700 miles of snowy wilderness, war zones, and corpse-littered battlefields. The party was once surrounded by angry French troops, ready to kill them as enemy Russians. Adams defused the situation by leading cheers for Napoleon in her fluent French.

The wife of foreign ambassador John Quincy Adams, Louisa would later become America's sixth First Lady. Hoping her journey and other risky endeavors would encourage others, she wrote:

"Undertakings which appear very difficult and audacious to my sex, are by no means so trying as imagination forever depicts them."

BIBLIOGRAPHY

Adams, Jerome. *Notable Latin American Women*. McFarland, 1995.

Bartlett, John. *Bartlett's Familiar Quotations*. 18th ed. Little, Brown, 2012.

Bates, Daisy. *The Passing of the Aborigines*. Pocket Books, 1973.

Blashfield, Jean. *Hellraisers, Heroines, and Holy Women*. St. Martin's Press, 1981.

Brakeman, Lynne, ed. *Chronology of Women Worldwide*. Gale Research, 1977.

Catherine II, Empress of Russia. *The Memoirs of Catherine the Great*. Translated by Mark Cruse and Hilde Hoogenboom. Modern Library, 2006.

Collins, Gail. *America's Women: 400 Years of Dolls, Drudges, Helpmates, and Heroines*. HarperCollins, 2003.

Crane, Elaine Forman, ed. *The Diary of Elizabeth Drinker*. University of Pennsylvania Press, 2010.

Dalley, Stephanie. *Mari and Karana: Two Old Babylonian Cities*. Gorgias Press, 2002.

Davis, Natalie Z. *Women on the Margins*. Harvard University Press, 1995.

DeLamotte, Eugenia, Natania Meeker, and Jean O'Barr, eds. *Women Imagine Change: A Global Anthology of Women's Resistance from 600 BCE to Present.* Routledge, 1997.

Ellis, Joseph. *First Family.* Knopf, 2010.

Fletcher, Joann. *Cleopatra the Great.* HarperCollins, 2008.

Forbes, Malcolm. *Women Who Made a Difference.* Simon & Schuster, 1990.

Fraser, Antonia. *Warrior Queens.* Vintage, 1988.

———. *The Weaker Vessel.* Vintage, 1984.

Goldsmith, Margaret L. *Christina of Sweden, a Psychological Biography.* Doubleday, Doran & Company, 1935.

Grace, Fran. *Carry A. Nation: Retelling the Life.* University of Indiana Press, 2001.

Green, Mary Anne Everett, ed. *Letters of Queen Henrietta Maria.* Nabu Press, 2011.

Grunwald, Lisa, and Stephen Adler, eds. *Women's Letters.* Dial Press, 2005.

Harris, Marguerite, ed. *Birgitta of Sweden: Life and Selected Writings.* Paulist Press, 1989.

Hervé, Francis, ed. *Madame Tussaud's Memoirs and Reminiscences of France.* Cambridge University Press, 2014.

Jones, Mary Harris. *Autobiography of Mother Jones.* Edited by Mary Field Parton. Dover Publications, 2012.

Keckley, Elizabeth. *Behind the Scenes.* Penguin Books, 2005.

King, Margaret. *Women of the Renaissance.* University of Chicago Press, 1991.

Knight, Sarah Kemble. *The Journal of Madam Knight*. Applewood Books, 1992.

León, Vicki. *4000 Years of Uppity Women*. MJF Books, 2011.

———. *Uppity Women of Ancient Times*. Conari Press, 1995.

———. *Uppity Women of Medieval Times*. Conari Press, 1997.

———. *Uppity Women of the New World*. Conari Press, 2001.

———. *Uppity Women of the Renaissance*. Conari Press, 1999.

Leonard, Elizabeth. *All the Daring of a Soldier*. Norton, 1999.

Moynihan, Ruth, et al., eds. *Second to None*. Vol. 1, *From the Sixteenth Century to 1865*. University of Nebraska Press, 1993.

Mozans, H. J. *Woman in Science*. MIT Press, 1974.

Murasaki Shikibu. *The Diary of Lady Murasaki*. Penguin, 1999.

Olsen, Kirstin. *Remember the Ladies: A Woman's Book of Days*. University of Oklahoma Press, 1988.

Partnow, Elaine, ed. *The Quotable Woman*. Vol. 1, *1800–1899*. Facts on File, 1995.

Perrottet, Tony. *Napoleon's Privates*. HarperCollins, 2008.

Royall, Anne. *Sketches of History, Life, and Manners in the United States*. theclassics.us, 2013.

Ryan, David D., ed. *A Yankee Spy in Richmond: The Civil War Diary of "Crazy Bet" Van Lew*. Stackpole Books, 1996.

Santa Lucia, Lynn. *Ladies First*. Metro Books, 2010.

Seidensticker, Edward, trans. *The Gossamer Years*. Tuttle Company, 1964.

Shelton, Jo Ann. *As the Romans Did*. Oxford University Press, 1988.

Showalter, Elaine. *A Jury of Her Peers*. Knopf, 2009.